A L

TO HIS GRACE

THE ARCHBISHOP OF CANTERBURY,

ON SOME CIRCUMSTANCES

CONNECTED

WITH THE PRESENT CRISIS

IN THE

ENGLISH CHURCH.

BY THE
REV. E. B. PUSEY, D.D.
REGIUS PROFESSOR OF HEBREW, CANON OF CHRIST CHURCH, AND
LATE FELLOW OF ORIEL COLLEGE.

SECOND EDITION.

OXFORD,
JOHN HENRY PARKER;
J. G. F. AND J. RIVINGTON, LONDON.
1842.

BAXTER, PRINTER, OXFORD.

In the interest of creating a more extensive selection of rare historical book reprints, we have chosen to reproduce this title even though it may possibly have occasional imperfections such as missing and blurred pages, missing text, poor pictures, markings, dark backgrounds and other reproduction issues beyond our control. Because this work is culturally important, we have made it available as a part of our commitment to protecting, preserving and promoting the world's literature. Thank you for your understanding.

CONTENTS.

	Page
INTRODUCTION.	1
Present Importance of Episcopal Charges.	3
I. Tendency to Romanism not produced by the Tracts for the Times; its real causes.	8
II. Recent Charges of some of our Bishops. Their effects. Review of them, as far as relates to the " Tracts."	39
III. Bishopric of Jerusalem; wherein an object of sympathy; wherein of apprehension.	111
IV. Conclusion. Recent aggravation of our confusions. Need of peace, sympathy, guidance; anxiety of present crisis.	136
Additional Notes.	163

May it please your Grace,

In times of less difficulty, it would be presumption in one in my inferior office to address your Grace thus publicly, without any hint from yourself: when the storm is upon the vessel, they to whom its guidance is committed, listen patiently to any voice, however humble, telling of some peril, which, from their position, may not be equally obvious to themselves. The greatness of the emergency excuses the boldness which it calls forth. "Suggestions, made even by the vulgar crowd, have been often profitable to the most perfect gladiators," is Tertullian's excuse for addressing those who were then occupying the fore-front of the battle, and soon to be enrolled in the "noble army of martyrs." Yet even thus, I can assure your Grace that it is with deep reluctance, that I have again come forward at all; much more, thus publicly to address your Grace and through you our other fathers, the Bishops of our Church. The natural repugnance which any one must feel at taking upon himself a task to which he has no apparent call, must be aggravated by the difficulties with which every thing is now encompassed. It is a far happier office to listen than to speak. It is painful to do what (notwithstanding all one may say) may *seem* like offering advice, when one had much rather simply obey, and where I *do* wish merely to furnish materials whereon you may exercise your own judgment; nor should I have done it, but for circumstances which I need not trouble your Grace by explaining. I quitted unwillingly occupations more congenial and more peaceful. Yet, though I have no title to address your Grace, your love of unity and peace, your anxiety for our Church, over which, by the grace of God, you preside, will dispose you to listen kindly to any thing, which may have for its object her peace and well-being; your condescending kindness, on different occasions, to myself makes it, I trust, less presumptuous in me to become the organ of offering it.

The ground then, upon which I am anxious to address your Grace is, (I may say at once,) my anxiety lest evil befal our Church, through an inadequate appreciation, on the part of those in authority, of the construction likely to be put upon what they do, and its effects. And in any thing which I may offer, I would wish to be considered rather as conveying information to your Grace as to those from whom your Grace's position necessarily separates you, than as venturing to offer suggestions as to the course which you may think it wise to pursue.

In the same way would I wish any observations to be understood which, in the course of this appeal, I may venture to make as to any thing, which I might wish had been otherwise, in any Charges of your Grace's brethren. I do not for a moment wish to criticise what they have said, in itself: I wish only to remark upon some probable effects of things so said, which they probably do not anticipate. And this, in every relation and office of life, we wish to know. Things which it may be right to say, may tell upon persons of different temperaments and tones of mind very differently. A kind master wishes to elicit from his servant the effect of his words, when he has occasion to find fault; else he may mistake silence for obstinacy or unconcern; a loving parent watches the countenance of the child he is blaming, catches gladly at its half-uttered explanations, softens his rebuke and soothes, so soon as he is sure that the effect is attained; all in secular authority, who have in any degree to guide by influence, wish to know how they are understood. Your Grace and your Grace's brethren are, according to your ancient title, our "Fathers in God;" and you would assuredly be not less anxious to know the feelings of those under your authority severally, and collectively under that of the body of which your Lordships are the chief; nay, rather the more, in that what is at stake is of so much more moment, the censure so much more solemn, every thing said or done affects indirectly the whole body of Christ; all relates not to time but to eternity.

Then, also, the circumstances of the times have given to the Charges of our Bishops a character so different from that which they had heretofore, that I may anticipate that the Bishops themselves would accept the more gladly any information as to the effects of them, which any might be enabled to offer. In quiet, one may say stagnant, times, such as until of late ours have been, a Bishop's Charge was listened to, one may say perhaps mostly delivered, with little interest; it was heard, perhaps read, in his particular Diocese; yet, unless for some incidental expression, but little noticed out of it, and then perhaps criticised rather than heeded. The Bishops themselves did not seem to expect much weight to be attached to their words; when they did rebuke, they expected to have persons of a refractory temper to deal with, and their words were sharp accordingly. Now, both within and without, things are widely different. The change of feeling with regard to the office of every one's own Bishop, wrought by more reverent habits, and increased appreciation of the feelings of Antiquity, gives their words a weight, of which they themselves are not aware: the relation in which they stand makes, as one of us feelingly said, "the slightest word of censure from one's own Bishop a heavy thing;" the very willingness to obey, the reverence and affection which we feel and would gladly testify, aggravate the weight of every thing which they pronounce against us, even as an affectionate child is more wounded by a look from its parent, than another by sharp rebuke or even blows. On the other hand, the intensity of the interest of the questions now at issue gives to every expression falling from your Lordships, weight and circulation among persons, who ordinarily would have thought too little either of your words or your office, at all events would have been out of the reach of theological discussion, for which they are little prepared, and which they now often enter upon injuriously. It may be among the manifold workings of God's Providence for our Church, that He has thus ordered that the interest of all should, in one way or other, be absorbed into these mighty questions. They have penetrated into our villages; they are the household talk of those who aforetime, alas! never spoke or thought perhaps of the things of God: all expect something, are on the look-out for something; that so the Truth of God may every where find its own; the good seed be carried, and root it in the clefts of the rocks, which it had never found, had not they who knew it not, dropped it unconsciously; all are somehow stirred and becoming alive to what is going on in the Church, that in every rank and sex and age they who may be won, may in this general preparation for His Coming take their allotted parts, await Him, live to Him.

And thus it happens, that every word of your Lordships, in the high office assigned to you, is watched and has a degree of weight given to it, proportioned to men's interest in the whole subject; they who at other times would slightly regard your words, now watch every syllable; they who would little regard them, if addressed to themselves, seize them eagerly as a weapon against others; they give them, I have reason to know, oftentimes a force which in themselves they were not intended to have; they who would take no other interest in them, use them now like moves in a mighty game, whereby they hope to obtain an advantageous position against those whom they oppose ; every word of censure or of warning is not taken as an insulated admonition in a particular case, but is made to bear upon the whole question ; it is a critical struggle for life or death ; and so, not a sound can be uttered, which penetrates not the whole frame ; every thing is strung up, and so every touch, sound, breath, motion, vibrates through the whole.

This, I think, some of your Grace's brethren have not, and, in the nature of things could not beforehand realize ; I have reason to know that one was recently surprised at the weight attached to his own words ; this must be the case, in some measure, with all in authority ; and the more, by how much more that authority is of a delicate and spiritual nature; our words,—as indeed the very word of God Himself, Whose word rebuke also is,— have weight according to the temper of mind of those they reach : but especially in a crisis like the present, in which the interest, month by month, becomes more extensive, pervading, intense, they who have passed most of their years in tranquil times, may well not be able to appreciate beforehand, what can indeed be adequately calculated by none. We are indeed altogether so little able to realize what we are ; that there may be no chance word or slight action of ours but may have its influence ; that a half-unconscious look or unweighed expression may leave a lasting impression on another's soul. And now every thing is new and on a new scale, and former measures will not apply to these times.

If then I express a wish that some of the language concerning part of our teaching had been in any respect different, it is because I am convinced that could the Bishops have foreseen its effects, they would themselves have modified it; nor yet do I write, as wishing that they should change what they have done, but rather in the hope that they who may hereafter speak, will speak, as in fuller possession of the manifold bearings of what they have to deliver. Recent circumstances present also a more immediate apology for thus venturing to allude to these Charges; for since others[a] have founded upon them an appeal to your Grace to " take such measures as may seem most advisable, for the Episcopal Bench to declare their united disapprobation of the opinions of the writers of the Tracts," it is natural for me to desire to shew that those Charges furnish no ground for any such measures, and to express my regret that the Charges of Bishops, who wished to warn, not to condemn, should yet have given such encouragement to those who would fain exclude us from our Church herself.

I. But before I enter upon the main subject to which I wish to entreat your Grace's attention, there is yet

[a] Address of certain Lay Inhabitants of Cheltenham. The example, I understand, has been followed in other places.

another point upon which it seems a duty to speak distinctly, however reluctant I may be, lest harm incidentally result, or I seem undutiful. Yet unless we know the true nature of our evils, we cannot apply their remedies; and so it seems to me very important that your Lordships should have a distinct view upon it, while yet I know that it is one upon which it is most difficult for those of elder years fully to understand the present state of things. That subject is the temptation to young or susceptible minds to forsake our own Communion for that of Rome. Your Grace will not think that in writing on this subject, I have forgotten what I have myself recently[b] said, as to the evils in the Roman Communion which should deter any from joining it, or the tokens of God's Providence which should bind us to our own Church, or the affection with which we should love her. But here I wish to speak on one subject only; the real, actual, temptations, to which *in the present state of things* a certain class of minds is exposed: and in that I say, "the present state of things," I mean that they are not inherent in our Church, but incidental only to her *present* condition; in that I speak of "temptations," I imply that it would be sinful to yield to them. Yet all would wish to know the temptations to which their children were exposed, and so your Lordships, as to your "children in the faith." In this case it is the more necessary to speak, on account of the difficulty of appreciating temptations

[b] Letter to Dr. Jelf, p. 159 sqq. and Appendix.

to which any have not been exposed, or to whose workings they have not been called upon to minister. Even those of my own age, who have been brought more into contact with Romanism as a living system than your Lordships, have not had the difficulties, which will beset many younger men; we have been brought on our way past middle life, and may the rather look to close it as we have begun; we have grown up thus long in our Church, and have, in such points as from circumstances are less distinct in her, gradually filled up her teaching to ourselves, by the teaching of the Church Catholic, of which she is the representative to us, and to which she directs her members; our insight into her teaching and Catholic truth grew together; we became more fully acquainted with both at once, and so they the rather harmonized in our minds. Our immediate Mother was our guide to "the Mother of us all." Romanism, in our earlier days, was scarcely heard of among us, and so we learnt Catholicity, partly as it had been handed down to us, partly from the study of Primitive Antiquity, not in contact with a system in which one must mourn that tares are mingled with the good seed. Romanism was, in our early associations, an antagonist principle; what is Catholic and true in it, we learnt, whence it is derived, from the primitive sources; of itself we thought, only for that which is peculiar to it, as distinct from Catholic Antiquity, the error mingled with the truth. It was apparently at a low ebb, and partook of the general listlessness which crept over the Church during the last century; it seemed to present but the skeleton of the right practices which it retained, and helped by its neglect of their spirit to cast reproach upon them; the writer of a work then popular[b] could even speak of it as extinct among us. It is not so now. The Roman Church also has, in some countries certainly, partaken of the same refreshing dew as ourselves; the same Hand, which has touched us, and bid our sleeping Church, " Awake, arise," has reached her also; our Lord seems to be awakening the several portions of His Church, and even those bodies which have not yet the organization of a Church, at once; it may be, that we may all together learn humility, and none boast herself, amid her imperfections, or think unhumbly of them, when she sees the like grace given to others, whose imperfections, as not being her own, she has no difficulty in descrying. However, whatever momentary difficulties it may give rise to, we must acknowledge thankfully that in England the Roman Communion has, amidst its sad errors from which it will not part, a degree of life and holiness which in our earlier days it had not. And this perhaps not least through an infusion of members of our own [now] who, in better times, would have remained, blessed and a blessing within her. She has now for many years exhibited her peculiar system in a modified form, the most calculated to win those who know not the treasures stored up for them in their own

[b] Father Clement.

Church. She stands too often in advantageous contrast, not with our Church as she would be, did we realize her gifts and avail ourselves of the privileges lodged in her, but with her condition, such as, through our sins and negligences, she has mostly become; and out of which she is beginning to be restored. The temptation comes not to those formed in the holy round of her daily devotions, and humbled by her tones of penitence, but to those, who through our carelessness have been unformed, untrained, uninstructed; or at least, are unacquainted with her true principles, the grounds of her claims, the virtue imparted through her. And to these the Roman Communion, as at present seen in this country, does come in a fascinating and imposing form[c]. She comes to us with our common saints, which modern habits have led many wrongly to regard as hers exclusively; with holy truths and practices, which in our recent carelessness are too often disregarded or neglected, or even spoken against amongst ourselves; with unity on truths, whereon we are distracted, (although, alas! upon doctrines and practices also which are not true nor holy;) with discipline, which we should find useful for ourselves, and which has been neglected among us; with fuller devotions[d], works of practical wisdom or of purified

[c] The following is not an ideal picture of what is calculated to influence; it is a statement of what I know to have influenced persons, and to be felt. I do not then suggest temptations, but state what exist. Temptations are to be remedied, not by denying their existence, but by a more vivid consciousness of duty.

[d] " There is so much of excellence and beauty in the services of

and kindled love [c]; a ritual, which (though withdrawn mostly from the laity,) still in itself at some holy seasons sets before the eyes more prominently than our own, our Saviour in His Life and Death for His Church, or which utters more distinctly some truths, which the sins of the Church caused to be more veiled among ourselves: or she points to a Communion of Saints, in which we profess our belief, but of which little is heard among us, now that even the prayer for the Church Militant for the most part, practically forms no part of our weekly service; she has, in her Monastic institutions, a refuge from the weariness and vanities of the world and a means of higher perfection to individuals, which many sigh after, and which might be revived in a primitive form, but which as yet we have not; in her small Communion in this country, she is not pressed on all sides by the spiritual wants of her children as we are, which hinder perhaps from noble enterprise in God's service, some who might otherwise have essayed it, still she does erect among us edifices to His glory, with which, notwithstanding the ample means at the command of

the Breviary, that were it skilfully set before the Protestant by Roman controversialists as the book of devotions received in their communion, it would undoubtedly raise a prejudice in their favour, if he were ignorant of the circumstances of the case, and but ordinarily candid and unprejudiced. To meet this danger is one principal object of the following pages." Tract 75. init.

* The use of French Roman Catholic books, in which the un-Catholic portion is very subordinate, has been one very frequent way of enlisting the sympathies of members of our Church, especially females.

our people, we have but a little, here and there, in this day to compare. Above all, she comes to us with her prayers; and some of her members by remembering us at the Altar, and night and day in the Holy Week, have drawn men's hearts unto them and won our sympathy and gratitude, in any lawful way wherein we may manifest it.

In all this, it is cause of thankfulness to see that there is nothing which ought to shake the stedfastness of a well-balanced and humble mind. Our duty is " heartily to thank our Heavenly Father for the state of salvation into which He brought us," when by Baptism He made us at once members of His Son and our Church, became Himself our Father, and gave us our Church for our Mother. Our plain duty is, " wherein we have been called, there to abide with Him ;" it is not for us to imagine, (as is people's continued temptation in every line and part of life,) that we should have easier duties and greater privileges, under circumstances in which God has not placed us ; it is, to be thankful and live up to our own, and pray that through our neglect or misuse they turn not to our condemnation. Were it even true that the Roman Communion did possess greater advantages than our own, this would be no practical question to us individually. It may be that one end which Almighty God has in exhibiting the Roman Church in this form among us, is to dispose us as a Church to more kindly feelings towards her, and to have a less overweening opinion of ourselves than we have mostly been wont to cherish. But individually it cannot change our duties. Our duties are positive and unconditional; they lie towards our Mother, the English Church, because God has assigned us our lot in her, and are irrespective of any thing without her. The duties and blessings of " the first commandment with promise" are in obedience to our Parent as such. Our duties are to her, because through her we were reborn, within her have we been trained, catechized, instructed, guarded, guided, called, recalled; in her words and in her Courts we have worshipped from childhood until now; in her we have had all our " means of grace," in her we have whatever be our " hopes of glory ;" at her breasts our Heavenly Father " nourished and brought us up[a]," as " children," and to forsake her would be to " rebel against" Him; through her He fed us, when young, with milk, in her He feeds us now with Angels' food, the Bread of Heaven; in her He has given us what out of her we could not have had ;—I need but allude to One precious Gift, whose value none can estimate, bestowed on us alone in the whole Western Church, and which I cannot understand how any Communicant who loves his Lord, could of his own act forego. One would not speak of persons in those Churches which refuse the Cup to their members; sore as the loss is, God can make up to His own, any losses which they sustain where He has placed them; but for

[a] Isai. i.

one who has had that privilege bestowed upon him, voluntarily to forsake the Communion wherein God has given it him, it does seem such a wilful rejection of the gift of his Saviour's Blood, as, in any who knew what that Gift is, one should dread to think of. And even besides this sad forfeiture, for any one, who, placed within a Church, has experienced God's guidance and the operation of His Holy Spirit on his heart, to forsake the Church, wherein God dealt so graciously with him, and shewed His merciful care for his soul— it does seem so ungrateful a disavowal of God's past mercies to him, such a cutting-off of all his past existence as a member of Christ's Church, as to make it very painful to think of those, who having been placed within our Church are being tempted to forsake, or have forsaken her who has the Apostolic Succession in this land.

But beyond these positive obligations, even in those things which in the Roman Communion are at first sight so attractive, what is Catholic and un-Catholic are so strangely blended together, that to any well-instructed mind, they create the longing to " re-appropriate [b]" what is Catholic, not to join a Communion, (itself, in this country, schismatic, and acting in a very unhumble and schismatic spirit,) where it is to be found only with what is un-Catholic. Throughout all she has of excellent, there is spread (to mention no more) that one corrupting leaven, the joining of the creature with the Creator, setting

[b] Tract 75, p. 1.

forth another object of affection, "giving His glory to another," teaching both saint and sinner to rely upon the Blessed Virgin as on Him [a]. This one addition, in itself, mars her books of devotion, her daily services, her Monastic institutions (which are in part instituted to promote it). One might add one error in practice,—withdrawal of privileges from her people; so that her Eucharists are to the majority mostly but to see the Heaven they partake not of, her daily devotions are no where given to the people, her most solemn service, that of the Holy Communion, seldom, but a modern service virtually substituted for it [b]. They speak of our service as

[a] To the sinner, as the refuge to whom he may most safely have recourse, as having the peculiar charge of " her goats," (all sinners who trust in her) as our Blessed Lord of the sheep, (Glories of Mary, p. 153, 4.) ; to the Saint, as obtaining for him that last crowning gift, perseverance to the end. The grace of perseverance is, in the received system, accounted to be specially obtained by S. Mary ; so that books, which have little else of the distinctive Romanist system, still teach to seek this at her hands. Thus this system proposes S. Mary as the immediate source of hope, from first to last,—of conversion to the hardened sinner, who has no other grace but love for her, (Glories of Mary, p. 40, 54—7, 90. quoted Letter to Dr. Jelf, p. 213. Man's only affair, p. 150 see Irish Eccl. Journal, No. 177.) and for the saint who needs no other grace but to persevere to the end. The evidence on both heads might be multiplied indefinitely. How different the teaching from that of the Catholic Church, as in S. Augustine de Dono Perseverantiæ.

[b] The most frequent way of " hearing Mass," as it is called, is to substitute other prayers to be used by the laity, while those in Latin are being recited, unheard, by the Priest. These are provided in different authorized books of devotion, so that many distinct Liturgies (so to say) are being recited at the same time;

diminished, (and in parts it is,) yet at least it is more than is given to their people. What we have (and it is very much) we have purely, and for all, for Christ's little ones, His lambs; what we have not, is being daily restored to us, if we in patience wait for it; and for the mean time, the humble-minded will feel that all which is withheld from us, is kept back in mercy to us, that what we have is best suited to us[b]. Such an Angel-life does daily Communion imply, that we may well think that it is too high a gift for the degenerate Church of these last days, as even the Roman Communion tacitly acknowledges, in that except for the Priesthood, she has herself disused it[c]; would one could think that

the modern mostly very inferior, and the ancient service virtually lost.

[b] To develope this is the object of Tract 86, "On the superintending Providence of God in the alteration of the English Liturgy." To some humble minds, who have ever enjoyed our beautiful and Catholic Liturgy, it will be painful even to hear it spoken of, as though we had lost any thing; yet we must " bear patiently each other's burdens;" and this Tract has been very chastening and sobering to many, who were inclined to mourn that foreign Reformers had been allowed an influence over it, and caused some things to be parted with, which we see to be in themselves a loss.

[c] Prayers even of the Missal are altered in the modern translations, to adapt them to a state of things in which the holy Mysteries are " witnessed" not " partaken of." In some places grave change of doctrine is thus introduced; as " May the mysteries we have *witnessed* purify us; and grant that this Sacrament [unreceived] may not increase our guilt, but be a means of obtaining pardon, &c. Let not the participation of Thy Body—which I, though unworthy, presume (*spiritually*) to receive, turn to my condemnation." (Catholic Hours, p. 96, 113.)

C

in different countries, it were a blessing even to them! As we grow in holiness, our present privileges will deepen to us, and we shall be fitter to receive whatever besides the Primitive Church had. Our blessings are, day by day, being enlarged; and He Who in mercy is teaching us to value and revive what we have, will, when it is good for us, restore what is yet " lacking [c]."

We may well be thankful that God has assigned us our lot in a " goodly heritage," wherein we are free from the temptation to substitute other objects of love or veneration for The Object Who is to fill the mind for eternity; wherein we are taught to "come boldly to the throne of grace," not seek another mediator, through whom to approach our Lord. We have or may obtain to ourselves when we will, every thing which is Catholic in the whole Church; our Liturgy has deep devotion, and is free from every thing un-Catholic. We may well shrink from parting with " the inheritance of our fathers," for its own sake, even if it could be done without sin. The path of duty is clear to humble and dutiful minds, who have ever been trained in the old ways; there are marks enough, we doubt not, for all, in the end, who in patience and self-discipline wish to know God's will that they may

[c] Bp. Andrews, Devotions, The second Day, " for the British, the supply of what is wanting in it, the strengthening of what remains in it." First Day, " Thou who walkest amid the golden candlesticks, remove not our candlestick out of its place. Supply what are wanting, strengthen what remains, which Thou art ready to cast away, which are ready to die."

do it. I am speaking only of temptation; what upon certain frames of mind would act as a trial, though to be overcome; but it is necessary to appreciate that there are temptations and trials; that the wish in individuals to be joined to the Roman Church, does not necessarily arise in undutifulness to our own, although one may generally trace some one wrong temper, at least, in those who have forsaken our Church for it.

And while there are these real attractions towards the Roman Church, (however more than counterbalanced in well-disciplined and humble hearts,) we must admit that there are also real difficulties in the position of our Church, which must be felt more keenly, as people realize more the doctrine of the Unity of the Church;—what our Lord intended that it should be, what it for a long time was. Not of course that these difficulties should overwhelm us; but they are hard trials to many, and must be accounted such, and borne patiently as trials. And in these again we ourselves have been exempt from the degree of trial to which a younger generation is exposed, through the very gradualness with which our conceptions of the Unity of the Church came upon us. There was in our younger days no visible Church, to which to attach ourselves, except our own. The Roman communion had in this country but her few scattered sheep, who had adhered to her since the times of Q. Elizabeth; she was herself asleep, and scarcely maintained herself, much less was such as to attract others. We were not tempted then to look for any thing but that invisible Unity, which we trust all the now-severed Communions have in their One Head, in Whom they all live, from Whom, though torn among themselves, we trust they are not rent. We dwelt alone, our island-situation a type of our Church, and were content, because there seemed no opening for any thing beyond. We were scarcely aware that we were rejected by the Western Church, not formally acknowledged by the Eastern, because we were locally separated from both. Girt round in our home, and living among ourselves, we felt not that we were regarded as aliens by those we saw not. We felt that we had, as we have, the Unity of the Faith, confessing to our God the one Creed—in our pious Bishop Ken's words, "the Faith of the Universal Church, before East and West were divided;" that we have the Unity of common descent from the Church which was one; we are one in one common parent, even if actual communion is suspended; one in the Communion of saints with the Church in Paradise, far larger and holier than that below; we have "one hope of our calling, one Lord, one Faith, one Baptism, one God and Father of us all;" through His Sacraments we "have been all made to drink into One Spirit," and so we the more acquiesced that we were one body, though some members of that body said to us, "We have no need of thee." But it is otherwise now; the Roman Communion is now every where among us, and we must feel that, if they could, they would cut us off; it is brought home to us that, from whatever causes, partly the sin of that first great schism of East and West, over which we had no control, partly through acts (whether they could be avoided or no) of our own Church, we are, as to actual Communion, separated from the rest of the Christian family; we feel ourselves in a maimed condition; our relation to other branches of the Church is different from any heretofore. There is no precedent in holier ages, either in favour of the larger branches of the Western Church, or of ourselves; none for such occasion of a single Church reforming itself, without consent of the whole [d], none for the larger Branch needing some such reformation and refusing it; rejecting one branch, and imposing un-Catholic conditions on its re-union. According as people contemplate the one side or

[d] The line, however, pursued by the African Church, under the guidance both of S. Cyprian and S. Augustine, goes as far to establish such a precedent, as can be furnished by primitive times, when no general reformation was needed. The case of S. Cyprian and the African Synods in maintaining the invalidity of Schismatical Baptism against the Bishop of Rome, is the stronger, because their view was not confirmed by the Church subsequently; the Bishop of Rome rejected their Communion, as he has ours; yet S. Augustine, while abandoning the practice of S. Cyprian, maintains against the Donatists, that he was not guilty of schism. In the case of Pelagius, the African Synods maintained their ground against Zosimus, Bishop of Rome, who acquitted him and severely censured them, and they obtained a confirmation of their sentence from the Emperor, to which Zosimus yielded.

the other, they will feel most vividly the fact or its excuse, and blame Rome for obstinacy, or ourselves for precipitancy; and since we have perhaps unduly held ourselves free from all blame, so the re-action is, that some are inclined to look on that alone which in us was blameworthy. Yet, besides the plea of necessity, the very unhappiness of the Church is our excuse. We did no act opposed to the Universal Church. There is now no orbis terrarum, over against which we stand; none which has rejected or condemned us. Since the Greek Church, and her ninety million, is severed from what claims to be *the* Catholic Church, and yet has life, so may we; and by the mercy of our God, we feel that we have it. It is a fact, that entire visible unity is not vouchsafed to the Church of these last days, and so, until God be pleased to amend it, we may rest contented in our lot. Yet the very fact that we have to be contented, shews that we have trials; our people go abroad, and find no home there; they see Churches, some flourishing, though some decayed, which, at best, own us but doubtingly; there is Christian life, from which we are excluded; the Church, the common home of all, is, out of the space occupied by our sister or daughter Churches, no home for us; they return to us, and feel that we are solitary. Then comes Rome among us, and,—rejecting the Greek Church of whose extent, as not being brought into intercourse with it, people are not aware, and so acquiesce in the excision of nearly half the

Christian Name as a light thing,—declares herself *the* Church[e], and offers to relieve our difficulties, and give vent to our sympathies, by placing us in

[e] This is the ground on which Mr. Sibthorp justifies his recent secession. He writes, as if unconscious of the existence of the Greek Church, as though the question were only between Protestants (with whom he has already learnt to identify the Church he has forsaken) and the Roman Church. In studying the types of the Old Testament he found the unity of the Church prominent, in a degree in which it is not in this day fulfilled, unless the Roman Communion be " *the* Church," and therefore he joined it. He unhappily overlooked that prophecy even more distinctly foretells " holiness" as a characteristic of the Church, in a degree in which it is still less fulfilled in the Church any where now. The same degeneracy of the Church forfeited both. Each is probably a condition of the other. Diminished holiness caused the misunderstandings and strife and ambition, which ended in the schism of the East and West; our schisms probably aid to perpetuate the unholiness which produced them. Life and desire of union are being reawakened together; increasing life will be accompanied doubtless with increasing love. But until the Church of Rome fulfils the ideal of holiness, set forth in prophecy, it cannot claim our obedience, on the ground that the ideal of unity, also set forth in prophecy, is not fulfilled unless she exclusively be *the* Church. If the sins of the Church have forfeited the one, they may also the other. It is a sad, but admitted, fact, that the Church of these days does fall short of the descriptions of prophecy. (see Mr. Newman on Romanism and Popular Protestantism, Lect. 8. Indefectibility of the Church Catholic, p. 231 sqq. who quotes also Leslie, Works, iii. p. 25—28.) The argument on which Mr. Sibthorp justifies his secession to Romanism, is the same in principle, as that on which the Donatists and many modern sects justify their schisms. They urged the non-fulfilment of the note of Holiness, as Mr. S. that of Unity. If holiness, the very end of the dispensation of the Gospel, may be imperfect, and the word of Scripture not be broken, much more may Unity. If the claims of the Donatists are not valid, neither are those of Rome.

communion with herself, the largest portion of the Christian world. And, since the desire of union is a right one, it is, when thus presented, a temptation, real, though to be resisted. We have, ever since we were thus severed, been feeling again after union; and this longing after it, although we could not attain it, may be a proof the more that we are a living, though torn, member of the one body. What is cut off has no feeling. It is, while the wounded limb still hangs on to the body from which it is disjointed, that it has pain. Sects have none. They boast themselves in their separation. Montanists or Donatists rejected the Church as carnal, and set themselves up as *the* one pure Church in its stead. *We* have ever missed more or less what we have lost, and have been yearning after the visible unity and intercommunion which we have not. Our very errors have been in part owing to it: we mixed ourselves up at the first with foreign reformations, and impaired our formularies, with a view to it; since then, our negociations with the Gallican Church, with Prussia formerly, with the Eastern Church, bear witness to our longings; at the beginning of this century, when wars kept us apart from other nations, and Church principles were less understood, this desire of union shewed itself in the very rejection of all true principles of union. Having no visible unity, people substituted an invisible; and not only so, which might have been right, but they sought to make a visible unity for themselves, by disparaging that of the Church, by sympathizing and associating with those who had forsaken her, and becoming like them. The same longing which some years past brought very many to the verge of Dissent, and often carried them into it, is now setting in towards Churches, and is a sore temptation to many to forsake their Church for Rome.

But, besides this, which is not our own fault but our unhappiness, over which we have no control, but for whose mitigation or removal we must in patience wait, it must be owned, my Lord, that we have other difficulties which are our fault, or rather that one difficulty, from which all others flow. Had we that holiness, which should mark us out visibly as a true living branch of " the Holy Church," all other difficulties would vanish. Now, we have, we trust, the rudiments of every thing, but nothing developed, so that it should at once be " manifest" to all, " that God is in us of a truth." " Whence come wars and fightings among you?" may the Apostle well ask us. These manifold divisions among ourselves, contending upon points which they on one side at least state to be fundamental, though *we* hope *they* believe better than they often speak; this bandying about of the name of heresy, and that, applied to holy truth, even the gift of our Lord to us in Baptism; this " casting out the names" of brethren " as evil;" this impossibility of understanding each other or making ourselves understood; alas! it is more like the confusion of Babel, when God hindered them from building the city, than that " city, which is at unity in itself," in which it was promised that there should be " one speech and one language." Our laity *thus far* have no living guide ; " the lips of the priest" do not, *thus far*, " teach knowledge," for them ; for persons, whom they alike respect, teach them differently, and one of the two great classes of teachers tells them often that the other is in fatal error. Those whom God endues with patience abide calmly, and in the Catholic teaching of the Prayer Book, wrought into their minds by habitual devotion, find that stay and guidance which the living Church should give ; yet can one be surprised that our poor frail nature is fretted often, instead of being humbled, by what is so unseemly ; that persons have difficulty in recognising a Church so disturbed, as the representative of her who is " the pillar and ground of the truth ;" that they should seek to escape this strife, by going over where they will find one who undertakes to guide them, allows them to surrender a judgment which they know not how to exercise, and to have peace ?

And in the comparison, which those thus tempted institute, our Church has this disadvantage, that our own evils are close at hand, open, plain to day. Those of the Roman Communion, in many cases, are veiled ; ours every where come to the surface ; the too sadly attested infidelity in southern Europe and France, might well more than counterbalance our dissensions or the imperfect belief of many; the superstition, or undue reverence, substituting the love of the creature for the Creator, too often found in foreign sermons in France, Portugal, or at Rome, might well outweigh any defects in our own; the violence whereby on the very Lord's Day, the passions of the people are in Ireland worked up by the Ministers of peace[f], and the obnoxious denounced from the Altar, might make the sad language against brethren or Churches, heard from time to time in our pulpits[g], seem a lesser evil; but their evils are less felt, because unseen, at a distance, unrealized, ours gall us, because they are our own.

Then, as to life. Our Church has indeed great difficulties, because it has an unruly, commercial, luxurious, unrefined, people to deal with. Antioch was, probably, of old in the most unfavourable

[f] The political meetings, at which so much inflammatory language is used by the Priests, are held mostly on the Sunday Evening.

[g] This has been a means of alienating people's minds to a degree in which they who use it, would themselves regret. If people are continually called Romanists, some will at length believe it of themselves. In a recent case, one, who would have been well contented to abide in the teaching of the Church, being told that she was a Romanist, and might as well join them openly, did so. To others, the question becomes very distressing, "How can I hold these high doctrines in my Church, who, they tell me, condemns them?" But, besides this, such language indisposes persons towards those who use it, frets them, and makes them sympathize even unduly with those against whom it is used.

position of all Churches, and we in many points too much resemble her. We must not visit upon our Church our national faults; but self-love blinds us to our own, makes us acute in seeing those of others. And so our Church bears the blame, if during the week, our churches stand empty, while foreign churches in the Roman Communion are full; and we her ministers are in part guilty, that fasts and festivals have been so entirely, and still are, neglected, that the daily service is but just struggling into use, that our Communions are so rare, our communicants so few, almsgiving so cold, luxury so rife, the very standard of our lower population as to one most debasing sin so miserably low, our sense of responsibility so little acute, the Presence of God so little habitually realized. Alas! my Lord, one need not go on with the sad catalogue; while we thankfully acknowledge that our Church has been an inestimable blessing to ourselves and to our people, and is capable of being far more so, did we carry out her provisions, and that the fault lies with us not with her, and that it will become otherwise when we in earnest wish it, we must confess that she does not in such degree possess the note of holiness, as at once and without all doubt to allay people's misgivings about her Apostolic character.

I have ventured to make this statement of some prominent difficulties, because, unless your Grace's brethren become more aware that there are real difficulties, they cannot meet them; one would rather fear that what they do, will be in a wrong direction. It is easy and not unnatural to ascribe the tendency to Romanism, which has of late burst upon us, to the influence of Tracts, which by those opposed to them have been accused of that leaning; but it would be a shallow and untrue account of the matter. We would not shrink from any blame which any of us may deserve; but when there is a general stirring, as there now is, through the whole of Christendom, it would be a superficial view of it to trace the workings in any part of the Church to any particular set of men or writings; we[a] did not set the tide in motion, by which we have been ourselves carried onward; we have felt that there is a higher Hand than ours, which has raised the waters and ruleth them; we are but one slight item in the vast sum, one link in the chain of causes and effects whereby He is working for His Church what He willeth.

It is important to appreciate this, my Lord, because if this movement were the work of our hands or the effect of any writings of any man, it might seem

[a] The use of this word having been misunderstood in my "Letter to the Bishop of Oxford," as though it recognised the existence of a party, it may be said, that here, as there, it is used simply as a compendious term for those who are attacked in common, for maintaining the principles of the Church. It is indeed not the least remarkable circumstance in the present restoration of our Church, how little of the character of a party attaches to those who have concurred in it.

capable of being stayed by the same means which produced it. It might suffice to warn against the tendency of writings which had called it forth. But now since even he who has been God's chief instrument has always insisted how little is his share; since every thing, good or evil, has contributed to it; poetry, arts, architecture, morals, Christian or Heathen, novels, music, painting, have either prepared for it, or, being subsequently absorbed into it, have swelled its progress; our renewed intercourse with foreign Churches and still more the evils aimed at our own, the suppression of our Bishoprics, the assaults of dissent, the coldness of adherents, the anger of enemies, the lukewarmness or hostility of the state, strength or weakness, loss or gain, the traditionary system, existing in our Church, though too often a dead letter, or the religious earnestness and life, though most opposed to that system, and, in its defects, to the truth itself—every thing deep, every thing real, every thing holy, deeds of charity, kindliness, severity, every temperament and habit of mind even the most unlikely, the most remote, or the most adverse, liberalism or sceptical tendencies, have alike ministered to it, it is plain that He Alone can have set it in motion Who Alone has all things at His command, and maketh every thing work together to accomplish His will. The tendency to Romanism, itself but one phenomenon in the manifold workings of this eventful day, is, as a whole, but a fruit of the deep yearning of the stirred Church to be again what her Saviour left her, One. Our severed members are being drawn to ourselves, as a Church, and knit into one in us ; as a Church, we are being drawn to other Churches, that, in God's good time, the whole body may be knit together under its One Head. Any deep view of the Church as one whole, must create a longing to realize what, as in vision, it beholds. Our severed state is a maimed and imperfect condition, checking, we must fear, the full flow of That Holy Spirit through our disjointed portions, Which, when perfectly present, makes what He pervades wholly one, even as He is the Unity of the Father and the Son. To feel what the Church should be, is to long that it be so. And if we come not with subdued hearts, settled to wait God's time for His gift, and anxious to take no step but just where He leads, there must be risk that persons will seek unity in unallowed ways of their own, and, as formerly with Dissent, so now in that communion which embraces the largest portion of Christendom, and which, in relationship as well as place, is nearest to us. This longing must be directed ; it cannot, ought not to, be quenched ; yet while it is active, (not to speak of other agents,) it were idle to think that any censure or silencing of men or books can stay what is the result of implanted sympathies, at the very centre of Christian life and love.

It may also be a relief to your Grace to know—it has come as a great relief to my own mind, since of late I have known it—that this confusion in which we now are, was not unforeseen. I mean not that it may not have been aggravated by any want of wisdom in myself or others; still it was anticipated as the necessary consequence of the restoration of the doctrines, which we have been employed to restore, before any of us were thought of as likely to be the instruments, or we ourselves had begun to look forward to the work, which has since been laid upon us. It will doubtless be refreshing to your Grace to see the words of one[f], whom in his inferior office, and as a Divine, you must have valued, how with the oracular prescience given to aged piety, when, as about to pass from this world, it receives, from time to time, a Divine insight into the things of that into which it is entering, he delineated in outline strangely faithful, the very form and order of things which were to be after his departure, but of which there were yet no signs. We may well be reconciled to troubles, which were thus marked out to us beforehand, as what we must necessarily pass through. And while we are thus content to bear them, and to be stigmatized as the causers of them and the " troublers of Israel[g]," they who are set

[f] Rev. T. Sikes, of Guilsborough, author of " Parochial Communion."
[g] 1 Kings xviii. 17.

over us may perhaps be the rather encouraged to bear their share cheerfully, and not be grieved at us, as if we alone by our errors caused, what, independently of us, it was foreseen would be. He, to whom the conversation was addressed, tells me, " I well remember the very countenance, gesture, attitude, and tone of good Mr. Sikes, and give you, as near as may be, what he said."

" I seem to think, I can tell you something, which you who are young may probably live to see, but which I, who shall soon be called away off the stage, shall not. Wherever I go all about the country, I see amongst the Clergy a number of very amiable and estimable men, many of them much in earnest, and wishing to do good. But I have observed one universal want in their teaching : the uniform suppression of one great truth. There is no account given any where, so far as I see, of the one Holy Catholic Church. I think that the causes of this suppression have been mainly two. The Church has been kept out of sight, partly in consequence of the civil establishment of the branch of it which is in this country, and partly out of false charity to Dissent. Now this great truth is an article of the Creed; and if so, to teach the rest of the Creed to its exclusion must be to destroy " the analogy or proportion of the faith," τὴν ἀναλογίαν τῆς πιστέως. This cannot be done, without the most serious consequences. The doctrine is of the last importance ; and the principles it involves, of immense power; and some day, not far distant, it will judicially have its reprisals. And whereas the other articles of the Creed seem now to have thrown it into the shade, it will seem, when it is brought forward, to swallow up the rest. We now hear not a breath about the Church ; by and bye, those who live to see it, will hear of nothing else; and, just in proportion perhaps to its present suppression, will be its future developement. Our confusion now-a-days is chiefly owing to the want of it; and there will be yet more confusion attending its revival. The effects of it I even dread to contemplate, especially if it come suddenly. And woe betide those, whoever they are, who shall, in the course of Providence, have to bring it forward. It ought especially of all others to be matter of catechetical teaching and training. The doctrine of the Church Catholic and the privileges of Church-membership cannot be explained from pulpits; and those who will have to explain it will hardly know where they are, or which way they are to turn themselves. They will be endlessly misunderstood and misinterpreted. There will be one great outcry of Popery, from one end of the country to the other. It will be thrust upon minds unprepared, and on an uncatechized Church. Some will take it up and admire as a beautiful picture; others will be frightened and run away and reject it; and all will want a guidance which one hardly knows where they shall find. How the doctrine may be first thrown forward we know not; but the powers of the world may any day turn their backs upon us, and this will probably lead to those effects I have described."

I would not weaken these solemn words by any thing of my own; but, my Lord, if it was foreseen that they who had our office laid upon them, would be " endlessly misunderstood and misinterpreted," that " there would be one great cry of Popery from one end of the country to the other," that they would have an office of trouble and " woe," that some would " be frightened and reject it," your Grace's brethren may perhaps the rather think that some of the things laid to our charge are founded on misunderstanding: if it was foreseen that it would be " taken up and admired as a beautiful picture," it will seem less strange, if some having done so, have fallen.

Yet, as a fact, I may mention, that both such as have actually gone over to Rome, and such as have been endangered yet retained, and those for whom one has immediate fears, have not been, for the most part, persons formed by any of us or by our writings. Those who have gone over, have been mostly persons, not at all instructed in the character of our Church, who sought in Rome what they might have found in our own Church, had they allowed themselves time to be instructed in her teaching; or they have been hurried by a violent reaction through finding the common-place statements as to Romanism so untrue; or disgusted by the vague charges and harsh or revolting language too often used[h]; or (from whatever cause) mostly out of Ultra-Protestantism, not at all from among us[i]. Every one

[h] Roman Catholics boast that the meetings of the Reformation Society are always followed by some secessions to them, and I am myself acquainted with instances of the irritating and unsettling effect of the vehemence and want of meekness too often displayed there. Mr. Sibthorp says, " I know not a Protestant controversial writer, (the authors of the Oxford Tracts alone excepted,) whose works did not leave me more a [Roman] Catholic than before." Some Answer, p. 36.

[i] Thus, to take the recent cases, of which this has been surmised, Mr. Sibthorp ascribes his late change to his study of the types of the Old Testament, upon which he entered when recently emerging from Ultra-Protestantism, (see Mr. Dodsworth's Letter

who has been at all consulted, knows cases in which persons who were going over from Ultra-Protestantism, have been thankful to be stayed, and found their rest in the true doctrines of our Church. I might say, that in any case which was not already gone too far, and in some which had gone extremely far, the true exhibition of the character of our Church, and their consequent duties to her and privileges in her, have been, by God's blessing, the effectual means of their recovery. Whoever have given themselves time to become acquainted with her, have rested in her. Those about whom we have had or have most reason to be anxious, have not been persons formed by our teaching, but are such as have struck out views for themselves, or have engrafted any thing we have taught, upon habits and thoughts which they had previously formed, or have been stayed for the time from Romanism by our teaching, or been acted upon by other influences and sympathies, or know no more of it than they who oppose it mostly do, gathering what they do know from common report, and carrying it out in an unreal and impatient spirit. I may say at once, that we have as yet no fears for those, who have been trained by the writings and teaching of those, whom,—one indirectly, the other directly,—God has chiefly em-

to Mr. S. p. 6—8.) An Oxford Tradesman ascribes his to his private study of Hammond, Thorndike, &c. the boy at Shrewsbury School was in habits of intercourse with Roman Catholics.

ployed to form men's minds within our Church, so long as that Church, by no overt acts of herself or her rulers, becomes other than she is.

And surely now, my Lord, when the very atmosphere is full of controverted doctrine, when the very periodical or daily press teems with discussions on the Church, Unity, Apostolical Succession, and, alas! on our holy Mysteries themselves, discussing all the details of doctrine or discipline wherein we are at issue with Rome; when people are taught by those most opposed to Catholic teaching to decide upon these points for themselves, and it is taken for granted that any one who has access to Holy Scripture is competent to decide upon them—it is too much to visit upon us any defections which there may be. Persons need not have recourse to the writings of any of us, to become familiar with these topics: I trust, that if they did, they would treat them with a more reverent spirit, and so more safely to themselves than is now too often done. It is not by us, that the young men in this place have now for some months had the subject of Romanism brought before them, or been taught to identify it with some whom they respect or love. The very clamour against "Popery," within or without the Church, is every where tempting persons' curiosity, and enlisting their sympathies; they who know nothing about the "Tracts" have their thoughts turned to Rome, and are interested in her, and study the works of Roman controversialists;

if they become bewildered, who should bear the blame,—they who inculcate the use of " Private judgment" or they who would restrain it[a]? they who enjoin obedience to the Church which has the succession from the Apostles, or they who set the individual's judgment as to Holy Scripture, above the authority of the Church?

It is not, as I said, my Lord, to excuse ourselves that I wish to impress upon the mind of your Grace and your Grace's brethren, a deeper view of the tendencies to Romanism than some of them seem to have taken; we have little to look for, except to finish our course, in sorrow or in joy, or in joy amid sorrow, as our Master wills; whether we have "honour or dishonour," will soon be no matter to us, save that we know that dishonour was the portion of our Master and His Apostles, and is the safer for those who would be His disciples. It is not for ourselves at all that I write; it is for our Church, lest she hereafter lose some of the

---

[a] See a very valuable article in the British Critic, No. 59, " On the use of Private Judgment," in which the writer shews that " Private Judgment" leads people *to* Rome just as much as away from it. The object of this Article is to shew, that the legitimate province of Private Judgment is to discover who is its authorized teacher, and that the English Church being such an one, " Dissenters ought to abandon *their* communion, members of the English Church ought not to abandon theirs." With this ought to be combined a previous Article by the same writer. Brit. Crit. No. 53, " On the Catholicity of the English Church."

flower of her sons; it is for them lest they be lost to the office which God had assigned them, and be betrayed into what would be undutifulness and sin. Unless our Bishops know the extent and character of our dangers, they cannot know how to guard against them; the very remedies they adopt may aggravate the disease, which they know not of. They may be applying stimulants, when they would, if they knew it, use lenitives.

II. And this I regret to say has been the result of the late Charges of some of our Bishops. It may seem, at first sight, undutiful, that the censures of Bishops should harass and cause impatience, and rather tend to unsettle persons in their Church, than convince and correct. It should be otherwise. But, my Lord, much confusion has arisen from people's forgetting that it is to our own Diocesan, not to other Bishops, that we owe obedience. All we should respect for their office sake, but it is to our own that we are to listen. It is, of course, a sad state of things in any Church, that they who should be overseers should need remonstrance from those in inferior office; but, not to go back to more ancient precedents, one of the most important controversies in our Church was carried on by a Presbyter against a Bishop, and succeeding Bishops could not but approve of the strong vindications of the principles of the Church by Law against Hoadley.

And this (painful as it is to allude to it) has

been the most distressing part of some of the late Charges. It is humiliating to our whole Church that persons who, in better days, would have been formed in the full possession of Catholic truth, should by our degeneracy have been thrown upon a system, in itself opposed to it, though neutralized in a degree by the influence of our Church. Yet it cannot be denied, that to those, unacquainted with the way in which that system is held in our Church, some of the Charges did, at first sight, seem to involve a denial of Catholic Truth. There is certainly in them a very inadequate statement of that Truth, and much which, to those not habituated to the mode of thought in the school in question, would seem a contradiction of it. But on this I shall have to trouble your Grace hereafter, in speaking of the Charges themselves. My object in adverting to it now, is to remove the impression of inconsistency, if they who have most vindicated the lawful authority of Bishops, should in any case be laid under the miserable necessity of speaking against what they deliver, or protesting against their teaching or their acts. I trust this may not be; but our duty to our Bishop is limited by his duty to the Church; he speaks to us as her representative; *through* her he received his authority, although *from* her Lord; his commission is to enforce her teaching, not to gainsay it; he received the succession from the Apostles, that he might hand down the deposit of teaching committed to the Church[a]; if then unhappily (as did Bp. Hoadley) he contravene his commission and her Articles of faith, it becomes a duty in any one, (while ready patiently to take any consequences,) to speak in behalf of the common faith. Our own commission, as Priests, is in terms as unconditional towards our flocks; " the Priest's lips shall keep knowledge, and they shall seek for the law at his mouth;" but if we go against the teaching of our Church, an appeal lies against us; in regard to a Bishop, the responsibility is the greater, by how much the confusion arising is the more sad; but his duties are the same as our's, our duty of protest the same as those of our flocks. I trust that, guided as our Church now is, no such unhappy necessity will arise; I would only explain how minds the most dutiful may be led to entertain these feelings, and be disquieted by the very shadow of so great an evil.

I may add that this duty of protest is not indefinite, nor another form of exercising " private judgment," but opposed to it; its subject is not what any may *think* Catholic truth, but the articles of the Creed. It was thus stated some years past; and this statement I may the rather cite, as shewing incidentally that it is not (as some, judging from their own principles, might be ready to suspect) an afterthought, provided to justify opposition to authority, if turned against us,—having been put forth contemporaneously with the inculcation of

[a] 2 Tim. ii. 2.

submission, and when it seemed altogether an abstract principle, least likely to be called, in this way, into action.

"As[b] they" [the world] "are eager to secure their liberty in religious opinions as the right of every individual, so do we make it every individual's prerogative to maintain and defend the Creed. They cannot allow more to the individual in the way of variety of opinion, than we do in that of confessorship. The humblest and meanest among Christians may defend the faith against the whole Church, if the need arise. He has as much stake in it and as much right to it, as Bishop or Archbishop, and has nothing to limit him but his intellectual capacity of doing so. The greater his attainments the more serviceably of course and the more suitably will he enter into the dispute; but all that learning has to do for him is to ascertain the fact, what is the meaning of the Creed in particular points, since matter of opinion it is not, any more than the history of the rise and spread of Christianity itself."

Thus, my Lord, while persons have been painfully alive to the character which might be insensibly given to our Church, yet, where deference might lawfully be shewn, from each to his own Bishop, censures, which I cannot but deem mistaken, have been borne very patiently. One of the Bishops who has thought it necessary thus to speak, has, I have understood, been much affected by the meek manner in which his reproofs were received by those whom they most wounded. But the body of the Church and those in whose behalf I am most deeply interested, have been

[b] Mr. Newman on Romanism, &c. Lect. x. init. 1837.

rather lookers-on than the direct objects of censure, and not having been subdued by personal pain, have been the more harassed by what has taken place. And that which harasses them is this. They have been formed or formed themselves in what we feel assured is Catholic teaching, in its main outlines instilled into us in our Liturgy and Catechism, taught in our Homilies, at the least consistent with our Articles, even where these are the least definite. This belief has become part of themselves; they cannot part with it, assured that God has given it to them through His Church, that it is part of the treasure committed to her keeping. Us (however unworthy such as myself, and however imperfectly any of us may have set forth that system) they look upon as its representatives in our Church. If then they who are in authority seem, from want of sufficient explanation, to censure our teaching broadly, it comes to them like a rejection of themselves from our Church. They find their belief disavowed, themselves disowned; whither are they to turn? It is not come to this yet; they who have spoken have been but a few; but it has been a distressing presage of what was to follow. "If all or the majority of our Bishops so speak," is their feeling, "will it not be a virtual disavowal of Catholic doctrine by the heads of our Church? And will it then be safe to abide in the Church, whose heads shall have so disavowed it?" This may be an undue anxiety about the morrow, and a mistrust of

God's Providence over our Ancient Church, which for so many centuries He has protected. I am not saying whether they ought so to feel; I am only stating what their feelings are. And to this they will ever be edged on by those, who are watching to take advantage of our perplexities. We are at a critical moment in our Church; every move is of an importance we know not of; and there is one at hand intently watching us, intent mostly on the destruction of our Church, and passing no movement by. I would request, in illustration, your Grace's attention to the importance given to the recent Charge of the Bishop of Durham in an article whose sole object is to add to the perplexities of those, who take an unfavourable view of the original structure of our Articles[k]. The immediate argument of the text relates to a distinct subject, the imponens of the Articles; I only allege it to shew how your Lordships' expressions are watched; and the note appended will shew one use to which the writer wishes to turn it.

"Are we wrong in supposing that a Bishop, making a Charge to his Clergy, speaks formally as a Bishop? If not, we would ask, when or how does he so speak, or when does he address the 'us' of the text, meaning, we suppose,

[k] Dublin Review, No. 21. p. 248, 9. It is a further illustration of the use made of these Charges, that the very title prefixed shews the existence of a spurious edition, "*Salutary cautions against the errors contained in the Oxford Tracts* [Tracts for the Times]. A Charge to his Clergy delivered at St. Nicholas' Church, Newcastle-upon-Tyne, on Monday, Aug. 9, 1841. By the Right Rev. The Lord Bishop of Durham."

the Clergy subject to him? If he does, then let us turn to the Bishop of Durham's Charge. 'And now,' it says, '... I must call your attention to the obligation which rests upon me, *your bishop,* on this our day of solemn meeting, *and to the manner in which you also are bound to act towards me,* who, however unworthily, am called upon thus personally, *and from the chair of office,* to address you.' (p. 3.) The Bishop, then, is about to speak episcopally, ex cathedrâ, as his own words imply. In page 6, his Lordship thus speaks: 'Strongly, then, must I repeat my regret, that with nothing like an appearance of stringent necessity, or the prospect of adequate advantage, *the writers of those Tracts* should have come forward to disturb the peace of the Church.' A Bishop formally speaking as such from the chair of office thus addresses his Clergy: 'A laboured attempt has been made to *explain away the real meaning of our Articles,* and infuse into them a more kindly spirit of accommodation to the opinion and practices of the Church of Rome. Under these circumstances, however painful may be the task of animadverting upon opinions espoused by persons otherwise so respectable, I consider it incumbent upon me *to pronounce my deliberate judgment.*' (p. 7.)

The note appended is,

" Mr. Ward has contemplated the course which an individual clergyman might be compelled to pursue, should his Bishop condemn the doctrine of the Tracts: 'It is, I suppose, considered by some that his Lordship (the Bishop of Oxford) decided ex cathedrâ, that such a mode of interpreting the Thirty-nine Articles was inadmissible; the result of which course would be, that those who held preferment in the diocese of Oxford, in virtue of subscription to them in such sense would, to say the least, be in a most painful position, unless they threw up such preferment." (Appendix, p. 13.)

I may add, that there are too many even in our own Church, who, little acquainted with our writings, and knowing us only from ex-parte statements and vague reports, are only anxious to see us removed, at any cost, from the Church. They have no thought of schism as a sin; they think of us but as a disease in the Church; and they only wish to see the Church set free from us, even though the act whereby it should be freed, were our sin. Or, having identified their own views with the truth, they are impatient of any thing which counteracts the exclusive dominancy of their views, and would be glad of any thing which would rid them of an antagonist principle; they would be glad to reign, if need were, without us, " vacua in aula," even though the Courts from which they would exclude us are the Courts of the Lord's House, the Temple to be left empty is the Temple of our God.

Your Grace will not think that, in expressing a wish that caution and tender care should be used, I mean to suggest any thing so unseemly as that our Bishops should not speak what to them seems necessary for the well-being of their Dioceses. If any think that we have wrought no good service, that all we have done has been in a wrong direction, such must condemn us. If any think we have " come forward to disturb the peace of the Church with nothing like an appearance of stringent necessity, or the prospect of adequate advantage[g],"

[g] Charge of the Bishop of Durham, p. 10.

or that the whole question is one about "antiquated ceremonies," he must think that we have acted very sinfully; and if he really come to this conclusion upon adequate knowledge of our writings, he must say so. My object in addressing your Grace is not to ask any thing of their hands who think of us as these must do, but of those who think that we have toiled faithfully and not altogether in vain, that when they censure what in us they deem wrong, they would not withhold the expression of their sympathy in what they esteem well done. Let them reprove, but in kindness.

I mean not to throw blame on what has been done, though I think it mistaken. I hope even that good may be brought out of it. One must even be glad that they who seemed most alienated from Episcopal authority, are now being won to it for the time, by its being apparently exercised in the direction in which they wish; hereafter perhaps the sounder and earnest among them may learn to respect it on higher grounds. It is very natural that, brief as our Bishops' Charges generally are, they should address themselves to the point which they deem of pressing importance. The Bishops seem to have had in view certain dangers from insulated statements; amid their many duties, some of them manifestly have not had leisure to examine as a whole the teaching upon which they had to speak. They seem mostly to have formed their warnings on detached passages, or, at the very utmost, insulated Tracts, without having time to enquire, whether one part may not have been corrected by another: they did not think it necessary to enter into the whole subject; they thought it their duty to give some specific warnings, lest they should seem to countenance what they do not, and so to leave the subject. On the other hand, the minds of hearers are more alive to censure than to praise; unhappily it interests mankind more; the detail, which it requires, fixes it more in the mind; and so it will happen, even if any services are acknowledged, the censure will be treasured up, the praise forgotten. The multitude is indiscriminating; too many are prejudiced, and interpret what is said according to their own bias. They know little or nothing of the system of which they speak, whether the censure, which they greedily repeat or inculcate, bear upon some doctrine or an individual's mode of stating it, or something only incidentally connected with it; whether it relates to some Catholic truth, or moral habit of mind, or mode of judging of other Churches, or of the character of individuals in our own; so that it relates to something in "the Tracts," forthwith, unless care be taken to express the contrary, they conclude that the whole tenor and substance of our teaching is condemned. And thus, even at the best, it will appear as if we were chiefly blamed, as if persons were being warned against our doctrine, and our view of our Church and her doctrines were pronounced to be at variance with her principles, when perhaps all which was intended was a caution against some insulated principle, as popularly misunderstood, or which we may have failed sufficiently to explain. Thus, I know that the mildest Charge which was delivered in the past year, and which does in a very kind way recognise services which we have rendered, yet, because the Bishop does go on to point out at greater length some, though fewer and subordinate, points which he considers erroneous, has appeared to be a condemnation.

The Bishop of Ripon says of us,

"In adverting to the opinions of those among the Clergy, who in their writings have advocated the restoration of ancient forms, it may surely be said, that so far as they earnestly call upon us to act up to the principles of our Church—to provide as much as in us lies, that she become in practice what she professes to be in theory—encouraging us to aim more fervently and resolutely at that high mark of holiness, self-denial, self-discipline, and almsgiving, which she holds forth to our view, and to live up to the elevated standard she sets before us, arousing us at the same time to a stricter sense of our accountableness to God, they deserve our honour and our thanks; still further I believe that they have done good service to the Church, in bringing forward more prominently some comparatively neglected truths with regard to the proper standing of the Church herself and her Ministers; as well as in leading some who were, perhaps unconsciously, inclined to view the Holy Sacraments as mere badges of the Christian profession, and the Holy Eucharist as little more than a commemorative rite, to entertain a juster sense of their real import."

This does indeed acknowledge the character of our efforts; this has been the object of our lives now these many years, to rouse our Church and ourselves to realize what she is in God's appointment, her Apostolic character, her high gifts, to stir up the gift which is in her, to act worthily of all God's past and present mercies. This is the ideal which we have proposed to ourselves,—not to alter any thing in her[h], but to recall the minds of her children to what she plainly has and teaches, and as occasion may offer, to develope according to primitive antiquity those doctrines and practices in her, which she has, yet, for some reason, not so explicitly as the rest. If I may address to your Grace, as a declaration of the principles and object of our lives, words which I have lately used[i], we have felt that

"We have our office plainly marked out to us, (as has been often said,) to labour to act up to the principles of our Church, and to lead others to do the same; so shall we be formed, and aid (under the Divine grace) to form others in the mould of " godliness, righteousness, and soberness of life," provided in her; we have but to seek to form ourselves and others in His holy faith and the keeping of His commandments, and commit our Church and ourselves to Him, to deal with us, as in His Infinite Mercy He may vouchsafe."

What we felt at the outset to be most wanting to our Church in her practical character, was what

[h] Letter to the Bishop of Oxford, p. 15—22.
[i] Letter to Dr. Jelf, p. 180.

the Bishop of Ripon has acknowledged in us. We did not wish to oppose any thing existing; we acknowledged, as far as it was true, the value and power of the popular system in its warnings against the world, its urgent calls to conversion, its pointing to our Blessed Lord as the Author and Finisher of our faith. But we felt it to be in part defective, in part erroneous; it laid the foundation, but too often neglected to build thereupon; it spoke of the Cross, but not of bearing it; it shrunk from inculcating "Judgment to come," "according to our works," the value of good works, of regular devotion, of self-discipline, of alms-deeds, and mercifulness; it but little appreciated the doctrine of the Sacraments, and therewith the mysteriousness of our life in Christ, our responsibilities, or the nature of repentance. Of the Church, as the mystical body of Christ, it had no thought at all. We set ourselves not to oppose, but to supply what was lacking, wishing not to irritate but to win; hoping that the exhibition of the truth would gain those who were susceptible of it, and that as it was received, what was erroneous would detach itself and sink of itself, even in the very process that what was true allied itself to the kindred truth, infused into it.

Truly and kindly has the Bishop of Ripon described our efforts to be, as far as in us lay, to call upon the sons of our Church "to act up to her principles," to realize the "high mark of holiness, self-denial, self-discipline, almsgiving," exhibited in her Liturgy, to "arouse us to a stricter sense of our accountableness," to "bring forward more prominently some neglected truths as to the proper standing of the Church and her Ministers," to "lead some to a juster sense of the real import of the Holy Sacraments." These were indeed worthy objects put into our hands, and all within the bounds of our Church—to realize our blessings, God's gifts, our own responsibilities, the high mark we are to aim at, the mode of girding ourselves to it, the account we are to give of all to Him.

But the Bishop of Ripon even goes further in detail; he not only incidentally says, "fasting and self-denial, when used as instruments of self-discipline to keep the body under, as a help to prayer—we know to be truly scriptural and Godly and edifying," whereas another Bishop[k] says of us, "The necessity of fasting is inculcated, and its merit enhanced too eagerly;" but even on the interpretation of Article 22, he sanctions the very distinction which I have endeavoured to draw out at some length, while other Bishops speak of our propositions having been authoritatively condemned[1], or say that for any to speak of the topics of that Article as only *condemned according to the Romish*

---

[k] Bp. of Durham, p. 24.

[1] By the four tutors,—" propositions, of which it has been well and *authoritatively* said." ib. p. 16.

doctrine[m] on these points," and otherwise admissible, " would, in a Clergyman, be departing from the sense of the Articles to which he subscribes."

The Bishop of Ripon, on the other hand, lays down the Roman doctrine, states it to be condemned, and implies that any doctrine different from this is not condemned.

"We must[n], as I conclude, in subscription to the Twenty-second Article, condemn the doctrine, that the sins committed after Baptism, even of those whose eternal punishment is remitted for the sake of Christ's merits, must be expiated, either by acts of penance in this life, or in a state of suffering and torment beyond the grave; this being, as far as I can collect, what is meant by the *Romish* doctrine of Purgatory; but I can scarcely suppose that any one ever imagined himself precluded by this subscription, from holding *any* opinion respecting an intermediate state, in which, *possibly*, the spirits of just men may repose from their labours *without suffering*, or indeed from entertaining any sentiment not included within the above definition of the Roman Purgatory. And so in like manner with the rest of the heads of the Article. Having ascertained what was the doctrine respecting the Invocation of Saints, to which the Church of Rome was held to be committed at the time the Article was penned, I should feel myself bound to subscribe in that sense, which I believe to be the legitimate and true one."

The Bishop's concluding caution,

"It surely can never do good service to the cause of that pure religion which has been committed to our keeping, to

---

[m] Bp. of Chester, p. 78, 9.   [n] P. 27.

speak in such a way either of this or any kindred practice, as shall encourage its adoption[n],"

is the very ground which induced Mr. Newman to speak so indistinctly at first; no one could warn more seriously[o] of the risk attending the resumption of any such practice; and his example has been followed by those who have since spoken, Mr. Ward[p] and myself[q].

Indeed, while the Bishop thinks it right to warn against the views of the Reformation and the Reformers, which have been lately more put forward[r], and regards the framers of Edward the Sixth's Articles as the imponents of ours[s], he sanctions *the* Catholic interpretation as much as ourselves. He objects only to the principle of arbitrarily affixing a sense which any one may *deem* Catholic; he doubts not, "knowing the respect in which our Reformers held Catholic Antiquity, that they correctly embodied that sense in them." On one doctrine only, does he remark on any of our doctrinal statements,—my own on Sin after Baptism; on one principle of practice only, that of " reserve as to the doctrine of the ever-blessed Atonement," on both which subjects I wish hereafter to say a few words to your Grace.

[n] P. 27.
[o] Letter to the Bishop of Oxford, p. 19.
[p] Few More Words in support of No. 90, quoted ib. p. 123.
[q] Letter to Dr. Jelf, p. 120, sqq.
[r] p. 20.
[s] p. 25.

If, then, amid all this, the Bishop of Ripon is counted among those who reject our views altogether, and condemn ourselves, what will be the case, if Bishops speak less cautiously and less tenderly? In these sad days of division and rebuke, every thing is seized upon as a weapon to demolish that which people dread; they look at things not as they are, but as themselves would have them; they value persons, things, institutions, according as they tell in support of party-views; a person or his work becomes at once, as it may be, learned or pious or judicious or venerable, as soon as he serves an end; they who never paid any respect to a Bishop, or who have spoken contemptuously of his office to his face, hail and extol his authority and magnify his sayings so soon as they are directed against what they dislike. All this is melancholy, very melancholy, and humbling, to ourselves and our Church in which these things are; but since it is so, I would the rather hope that they whose words will be so employed, will consider the more the weight of sayings, which are so to be employed, that they press not the heavier against those already bowed down.

Will your Grace permit me to illustrate my meaning by reference to an older Charge, which went more into detail into our doctrines than any other at that period? In 1836 the Bishop of Exeter laid down, with his usual perspicuity, the doctrine of the Sacraments and of the Eucharistic Sacrifice, and the latter in terms which struck myself as so happily chosen, that we added it to our Catena on the subject, instead of closing it with departed Divines. In 1839 he again stated the teaching of the Church on the Apostolical succession, and on the doctrine of the Sacraments in the same manner as we ourselves would do; on the Holy Eucharist, he maintained the right use of a term not contained in our formularies, the "real Presence," which I am not aware that any of us had used; again setting us an example, not simply sanctioning what we had taught. On Tradition again, the Bishop affirms its value,—especially wherein it comes to us with chief authority, the Creeds,—and subsequently objects to individual expressions only of ours, which he thinks to magnify it too much, while he rejects the charge of Popery brought against us, and very severely that of heresy. When he is subsequently led to point out some things which he laments, they are still points of detail; of a mode of speaking of worship of images and invocation of saints less marked than Bishop Hall's; dislike of making Transubstantiation a subject of controversy; my own defence of the practice of prayer for departed Saints; the service sketched in commemoration of Bishop Ken; speaking against the *necessity* of Confession as a "practical grievance," without saying any thing against the Roman statement of the absolute necessity of Absolution by the Priest; my own views of sin after Baptism; reserve on the doctrine of the Atonement. Without entering into these manifold subjects, the very enumeration shews that most of them are negative only; the degree of blame attaches mostly to what we did not, and not to what we did say or do; one point only is connected with our positive practical teaching,—my own on sin after Baptism;—for although, when blamed as we were, we must maintain Prayers for departed Saints to be a Catholic practice, we never publicly inculcated it. I mean not that the Bishop might not object to other of our language, were he acquainted with it, but he did censure no more. He even concluded his animadversions upon these points with the kind parting words.

"Neither[q] shall I forbear to avow my own opinion, that the Church is on the whole deeply indebted to them.

"In opposition to the low and sectarian notions, which had too long marked much of the popular theology of the times, they have successfully asserted and vindicated some of the most important doctrines and principles of the Catholic Church—doctrines and principles, which, as Ministers of that Church of England, we are under the most express and solemn engagements to maintain."

Yet the Bishop of Exeter also has been alleged in the catalogue of those who have condemned us, and we have been represented as contumacious in continuing to teach, after having been thus rebuked; and that by those, who unhappily seem to deny what the Bishop designates as " some of the most

[q] p. 84.

important doctrines and principles of the Catholic Church," and which he holds that as Ministers of our branch of the Church we are most solemnly bound to teach.

But if this be so as to those who have spoken thus kindly of us, what must be the impression made by such as simply censure us without adverting to any good service we have rendered? Thus, the impression left on my mind by a Charge delivered in the foregoing summer by an Archbishop of the United Church was, that he held that we ought to leave the Church,—meaning probably, abandon our office as Ministers in her. The Bishop of Durham expressly says that we have done no good, that there was no need and no excuse for our efforts, nothing in the existing state of doctrine to call them forth, that the result of our efforts has been very unfortunate, tending to reestablish error rather than truth. The Bishop of Chester seems (shocking as it is to write) to regard us as instruments of Satan to hinder the true principles of the Gospel[a]; his brother, the Bishop of Winchester, speaks more mildly of us, condemns nothing authoritatively, yet sees nothing but evil from us, and no evil except from us[b]; an

---

[a] See an extract in Note A at the end.

[b] " Are we, then, as a Church, in risk of incurring any such danger?" [being robbed of her internal and spiritual beauty and strength,] " Is our glory in any jeopardy? Is there heard, as it were, something of a confused sound of voices at a distance,

Episcopal Sermon, delivered indeed in much excitement[c], and which has been reprinted here from a Colonial Diocese, as an additional weapon against us, speaks of us as on " the very verge of an apostasy from Christ[d]," meaning indeed thereby an approximation to Rome.

And yet, my Lord, even of these last, (sorrowful as it is to be mistaken by such men,) I would without hesitation affirm that they mostly condemn not ourselves or our principles, but what they conceive to be such. I may say this the more confidently, as having, now these many years, read diligently what has been written against us, and seen how impossible it is to convey to minds, trained in one school of theology, the real character of views at variance with their own. It has been my own lot, as well as that of others, continually to see and hear ascribed to ourselves views and statements, the very reverse of any

---

which might make some Eli, sitting in the gate, to tremble for the ark of God? If there be in the horizon so much as the earliest rising of a little cloud, you have a right to expect from one in the position which the duty of my office bids me discharge this day, the explicit declaration of my fears." Charge, p. 29. and then he proceeds to speak of what he supposes to be our teaching, and of our's only.

[c] " I am full of fear; every thing is at stake." " I am an alarmist. I believe our Church was never in the danger she now is, except perhaps immediately before the Great Rebellion." i. e. (as it is explained) from Abp. Laud. Ordination Sermon by Daniel Bishop of Calcutta, p. 63, 64, 65.

[d] p. 61.

which we hold. It is even shocking to have to deny or to affirm, respectively, the grievous errors or the elementary Christian truths which it is supposed that we should hold or reject. As a rule, we should be found to reject what we are by this class of minds thought to hold, to hold more nearly what we are thought to reject.

This has arisen out of the circumstances attending the revival of religious earnestness towards the close of the last century. The instruments of that revival looked, in the first instance, for the type of their doctrine, neither to the Reformers of the sixteenth, nor the great Divines of the seventeenth century, but to the Non-conformists. In contrast with a period in which the consciousness of the great truths of the Gospel had become obscure and dim, they seized, as your Grace knows familiarly, one or two fundamental truths, or rather they condensed the whole Gospel into the two fundamental truths of nature and of grace, that by nature we are corrupt, by grace we are saved. Our corruption by nature, our justification by faith were not a summary only, but, in this meagre form, the whole substance of their teaching. Faith also was made the act of the mind, believing and appropriating to itself the merits of our Blessed Lord; the rest of the Christian system or God's gifts, the Church, the Sacraments, good works, holiness, self-discipline, repentance, were looked upon but as introductory or subsidiary, or to follow as a matter of course upon these, but if thought of any value in themselves, pernicious; to attach value to any of them, was (as we have often been condemned to hear, and shocking as it is to repeat) to substitute (as it might be) the Church or the Sacraments, or repentance or good works for CHRIST. And from this we are but partially recovering. One must respect the sensitiveness of those, who with a " godly jealousy," fear lest any thing be substituted for our Ever-blessed Redeemer. Still one must say that the error is with them. The narrowness of what one must call the " Non-conformist" system (for on the doctrine of Holy Baptism it is plainly at variance with that of the reformers in our Church as well as its formularies) cannot span the largeness of Catholic truth; it cannot expand itself so as to comprise it, and what it cannot take into its own measures, it rejects as superfluous. Measured then by this rule, our teaching must needs be found faulty.

I may the rather venture to say this, my Lord, without arrogancy, because it is difficult to see how one at least of these Charges can otherwise be reconciled with the formularies of our Church, or even the Creeds of the Church Catholic: it is no disrespect to speak of the unclearness or narrowness of a system, even when adopted by a Bishop; it were shocking to think of any thing approaching even to unconscious heresy. If then "justification by faith only" is used to exclude any thing else as the *meritorious* cause of our salvation, than the merits of our only Lord and Saviour[g], it is, of course, only a brief statement of the whole substance of the Gospel. In this sense it is right to be jealous for the doctrine, and in this the Bishop of Chester must be understood[h] when he condemns as " departing from the sense of the Articles" any who " speak of justification by faith, as if Baptism and newness of heart concurred towards our justification[i];" for to deny in any other sense that Baptism concurred to our justification would be to contravene Holy Scripture, as well as the Creeds and the

[g] " Then will His Cross and Passion again be known, beloved, acknowledged, relied on, gloried in, as the *only meritorious ground of justification*, and His Spirit sought for and honored, as the *only gracious source of holiness and comfort.*" Bishop D. Wilson's Charge, p. 69. The Italics are the Bishop's. There must be some miserable confusion when a Bishop could suppose that such elementary truths were not held by any teachers of the Church.

[h] I know not whether it is in the same sense that the Bishop of Winchester expresses his " fears of a system" " which speaks of the Sacraments, not as seals or pledges, but as instruments of salvation in a *justificatory* or causal sense;" for I do not understand what it means. Our passages, to which the Bishop refers, speak of the Sacraments only as " instruments;" an instrument is, in scholastic language, " the immediate cause," (as distinct from the " ultimate cause" or Author,) as our Article also speaks of their being " effectual signs of grace," i. e. effecting what they signify; and of Holy Baptism as " an instrument whereby they who receive it rightly are graffed into Christ's Church." But what " an instrument in a *justificatory* or *causal* sense" is, I know not.

[i] Charge, p. 79.

formularies of our own Church[i]. For in that Holy Scripture, and the Creed after it, speaks of "Baptism for the remission of sins," Baptism must concur to justification, or our being made free from sin; and, (on the narrower ground of our own formularies,) in what other way could each be taught to say that he was "therein made a child of God, member of Christ, inheritor of Heaven?" unless, indeed, a person can have all these glorious gifts and testimonies of God's mercy, and yet be unjustified and lying in his sins, and under God's wrath,—an unjustified "child of God, member of Christ, heir of heaven!"

It is probably in this same sense that the same Bishop condemns those who "speak of Forgiveness or works of mercy, as availing to obtain remission of sins from God;" i. e. (he must mean) meritoriously or in themselves, (which no one affirmed,) else he would contradict Holy Scripture, which says, "Forgive[k], and ye shall be forgiven;" and "When[l] ye stand praying, forgive, if ye have ought against any, *that* your Father also, which is in Heaven, may forgive you your trespasses;" and "He[m] shall have judgment without mercy that hath shewed no mercy, and mercy rejoiceth against judgment."

[i] See more at length Mr. Perceval's well-weighed "Letter to the Bishop of Chester, with remarks on his late Charge, more especially as relates to the doctrine of Justification."
[k] Luke vi. 37.
[l] Mark xi. 25.
[m] James ii. 13.

Again, when the Bishop of Winchester expresses his "fears[n]," " if instead of the satisfaction of Christ singly and alone as the ground of our acceptance, a certain inherent meetness of sanctification be so connected with the qualification ab extra, as to confound the operation within with the work of Christ without;" if he means " the *meritorious* ground of acceptance," no one of course holds any thing else; yet he cannot mean to deny altogether that any other ground shall, in any way, be taken into account in the final "acceptance" at the last Day, since our Lord declares that works of mercy will[o].

In like way, one may say of these Charges throughout, that the writers are jealous for truth, or against error, which all earnest minds must be jealous about; only they seem to have these truths fixed in their minds in the (one may say so without disrespect, as speaking of the system, not of the respected individuals) somewhat bald and naked way which characterizes the Genevan school, and measuring doctrines as they stand in other systems by the character which they would occupy in their own, they must condemn them. And thus they might too readily be understood to be condemning, not our teaching only, or that of the great Divines of the seventeenth century, but that of our Church and the Church Catholic, and to be at variance

[n] p. 30.   [o] Matt. xxv.

with Holy Scripture. Their chief maxims, that nothing must interfere with the office of Christ, or derogate from the sufficiency of Holy Scripture, all would hold with them, but in the application of these principles, they seem not only to condemn other truth, but even to contradict themselves.

Thus the Bishop of Chester descends even to controvert the thoughtful work of an eminent layman, who has recently developed the doctrine of the mystical character of the Church; and in his anxiety that the Church should not be " made to usurp the place of Christ to perform His acts," so pares down the doctrine, as to seem to leave the Church a mere outward body composed of such as (using an illustration from a regiment°) " vow allegiance, and pass through a prescribed form, such for example as Christian Baptism," a body as merely outward as a regiment might be, as not in fact one body, except as an accidental aggregate of individuals can be said to be one. And yet such cannot be his meaning, since though the language of the Article which he quotes is ambiguous, that of our Services falls in with and implies the view which he seems to controvert, that the Church is a mystical body into which they who are saved are gathered one by one, and in it knit to Christ, its and their Head. This is plainly the meaning of our Liturgy when it speaks of " God's elect" being

° p. 84 sqq.

"knit together in one communion and fellowship in the mystical body of His Son Jesus Christ," or of our being assured by the due reception of the Holy Eucharist, "that we are very members incorporate in the mystical body of His Son;" of children "being received into Christ's holy Church," by "being baptized with water and the Holy Ghost," "received into the ark of Christ's Church," being "regenerate, and grafted into the body of Christ's Church," "regenerated by God's Holy Spirit, received as His own child by adoption, and incorporated into His Holy Church." The body into which we are engrafted by the spiritual gift of our new birth must itself be spiritual. Such an outward view of the Church would be inconsistent with the Creed itself, "I believe The holy Catholic Church;" for which the Lutherans, on their view, substituted the words "*a* Christian Church."

Yet it is apparent throughout that the Bishop only means to contend against what all would equally reject—any view of the Church which should substitute it for Christ, one which would "so[p] represent it, as to be virtually the author of salvation, instead of the channel through which salvation flows;" although (remarkably enough) the passage from Mr. Gladstone's work which he cites in illustration, does distinctly speak of the

[p] p. 30.

Church, not (it is almost too shocking even to deny) as the Author but as the channel[q]. It is apparent even from the Bishop's own language, for he too speaks, with Holy Scripture, of the Church, as one spiritual body under Christ its Head.—" The[r] Holy Catholic Church, of which Christ is the Head, and with which He has engaged to be by His Spirit unto the end of the world."

I do not mean that there is not a real difference of view between their statements and our own; but it proceeds from defect and omission in theirs, not from direct opposition; ours supply what they omitted, and so, as long as they are satisfied with their own, ours must seem to them redundant. Raised up at a time when the Christian Sacraments were acknowledged but not felt, they took up a system independent of them; they urged conversion, they proposed justification, not by virtue of a Covenant which had been neglected, an en-

---

[q] " It is in the Church that we have our religious life, *derived to us not as individuals, but by virtue of incorporation into her body.*" " God has not chosen to establish His relations with each of us on a distinct and individual footing, but has constituted us in a body, to derive *from its source of life* a portion of its general life." quoted ib. p. 80. The same contrast is observable in all the Bishop's subsequent remarks; as in the saddening words, p. 81, " Shall we write, instead, Come unto *the Church*, and *the Church* shall give you rest?" " Shall we substitute the Church Catholic for the individual Saviour?"

[r] ib. p. 33.

grafting into Christ whose efficacy had been stifled, but de novo, as if every thing past were effaced; as if a man had had no privileges, responsibilities, duties, because he had neglected them. Overlooking the Ordinances whereby God engrafts us into Christ's body, they addressed men as individuals, now for the first time, through their individual faith, to be united to Him; and they the more depreciated His Ordinances, because others urged them to a wrong end,—to supersede the necessity of any actual change, any decided living above the world, or contrast with its ways. They called men who were *in* the Church, as the Apostles called them *into* it; and so must needs overlook the Church herself and the Sacraments whereby men had been brought in; they took one half only of the truth, viz. that the individual must by his personal faith cleave unto his Lord, and overlooked that no human faith nor longings can make a man a member of his Incarnate Saviour, that they only can be united with Him, whom He receives into His mystical Body, and that this His act is the Sacrament of Baptism. They insisted rightly, against the prevailing coldness, on the necessity of individual personal faith, they substituted wrongly the act of man for the Sacrament of Christ; they insisted rightly on the individual relations of the believer to Christ, but failed to perceive that these relations were no less individual, because they belong to us as members of the one Body, whereof

He is the Head. And thus, so long as they teach positively, all can accord with them; when they go beyond it, they seem to oppose Catholic truth as well as our teaching. They have realized the one truth of the individual union with Christ; when they hear of the Catholic doctrine of the Church and of the Sacraments, they know not how to reconcile them with their own partial views, they fear something being " interposed" between the soul and its Redeemer, and so seemingly reject the truth, when they really reject but a partial view of it, which would be destructive of other truth.

It is important, even at the risk of being wearisome to your Grace, to trace this source of apparent opposition in other points, if so it may appear not only that we are not so condemned, but that the points upon which the teachers of our Church are at strife are not, if we rightly understood each other, so numerous as might at first sight seem. Thus, on Tradition, these writers are very jealous for the sufficiency of the Scripture, and too much of course could not be said on that subject, unless in so doing men should seem to praise the word of God. All hold Scripture to be the "sole source of saving Faith;" the only question is about its interpreter, whether it be the individual or the Church. There is no contrast in the mind of any maintainer of Tradition, between Tradition and Holy Scripture, and yet this seems the only contrast in the mind of pious men who impugn it. I say "of pious men," for too many in these days are anxious to maintain not the independence of Holy Scripture, but their own. And thus it will be that these writers will seem alternately to affirm or condemn, what they condemn us for affirming. Thus the Bishop of Calcutta says, as do we, that it is the office of the Church " to uphold[*] the word of truth, to be the keeper and guardian of Holy Writ—to explain it by comments, creeds, liturgies, articles, and catechisms, and hand it down to successive generations. By these means truth resides in the Church as its fixed seat and proper dwelling." When he adds, " all as a servant, as a handmaid, not as an authority over or co-ordinate with Holy Scripture," he speaks only as we do, who regard the Church as subservient to Holy Scripture; having " authority" not " over" *it*, but " over" *us*. When, further, he adds, the office of the Ministry is to " interpret merely, not change or add to, much less explain away or contradict. The standard of all religious teaching is the Bible and the Bible only ;" this is, again, what we should say, if by " standard" he means the *ultimate* authority to which the Church is to appeal. When, again, he says, " We[†] go along with the most ardent admirer of Antiquity in expressing our reverence for this mass of information," [Fathers, Councils, &c.] But why ? It is EVIDENCE ; it is historical testimony to the fact of certain

[*] Sermon, p. 24.
[†] p. 28. The Capitals are the Bishops.

doctrines, and a certain interpretation of the capital leading passages of Scripture, of a certain number of sacraments, rites, and usages, having been held in all ages, in all parts of the Church and by all persons;" this is what we have said, " Scripture" is the document of faith, tradition the *witness* of it; the true Creed is the Catholic interpretation of Scripture, or Scripturally proved tradition." Whatever difference there is, relates not to the sufficiency of Holy Scripture in any way, nor to its being the sole source of saving faith, nor to its superiority to man, nor to its authority over the Church; it relates not at all to Holy Scripture but to *us*; not to the sufficiency of Holy Scripture but to *ours*; not to submitting Holy Scripture to the Church Catholic, but *ourselves*; not whether tradition is equally inspired with Holy Scripture, but whether we are equally enlightened and have as much of the Spirit of God, and as much insight into Holy Scripture itself, as the collective wisdom of the Church; not whether the Church has authority over Holy Scripture, but over us; not whether it may " change or add to, explain away or contradict" Holy Scripture, but whether we may " change, explain away, or contradict" the decisions of the Catholic Church. The whole question of tradition relates not to Holy Scripture, but to the individual; and what many who impugn it are half-consciously con-

* Tract 78, p. 2.

tending for, is not the sufficiency of Holy Scripture, but the sufficiency of self. This is a question which will probably be more and more developed; there are who contend that the later ages are in religious wisdom richer than the earlier; the stream purer as it flows downwards; the division of these last times more enlightened (and more loving doubtless, and more enlightened because more loving!) than the unity of the first; and so criticism too, doubtless a better guide to " the mind of Christ" than holiness, the decay of the Church more guided by her Lord and blessed with His fuller Presence, than her first love. But, apart from this, the struggle which is being carried on every where, and which is the characteristic contest of the " last times," is that between the individual will and authority; it pervades politics and religion; without the Church it is the question of submitting the reason to mysteries, " the prostration," as your Grace once spoke, " of the understanding" before revelation; within, it is of the submission of the individual judgment to that of the Church. This is a question of religious temper of mind, of first importance; and there are symptoms even within the Church that this struggle is being secretly carried on, under the fair colours of zeal for the " sufficiency of Holy Scripture;" it is to be feared that when the right-minded understand each other better, the mask will be drawn aside by those who are not so, and the untruth avowed more nakedly; it is one of the signs of the last Apostacy; but it is happily not at issue between these Bishops and ourselves.

In other points again, the Bishop of Chester shews what the error is which he means to condemn, and so, though he rejects statements, which are borne out by Catholic consent, there is no reason to infer that he rejects the truth they contain, but only the error, which though they do not, he supposes them to maintain. Thus it was part of the vague way of thinking in a past period, to suppose that *any* change in the sacred elements involved Transubstantiation, whereas that word designates only that particular change, " whereby the substance of the sacred elements ceases to be." When then he condemns[x] as " departing from the sense of the Articles," those who " speak of the consecrated elements as not remaining simply what they were before, and what to sight they seem," and refers, as his authority, to the Article condemning Transubstantiation, we may plainly limit his condemnation to this, and not suppose him to contravene Antiquity, which continually affirms *a* change, as indeed it is implied by the prayer for the descent of the Holy Ghost in all ancient liturgies except the Roman, and by the very act of consecration.

Or, to speak on one subject which has been perhaps more widely misunderstood than any other,

[x] p. 79.

(though not a doctrine,)—" reserve" or reverence "in communicating religious knowledge,"—the principle of the tracts on that subject, (of which an impartial person has said that " they contain as much deep and true philosophy as any in the whole series,") may be expressed in few words : " great reverence is to be used lest you propose religious truth to minds unfit to receive it." Whatever rule as to holy truth is meant by our Blessed Lord's words, " Give not that which is holy to dogs, nor cast your pearls before swine," that and no other is meant by these Tracts. This is contrary not (God forbid) to the preaching of the Atonement, but to a sadly irreverent way of preaching it, as the means of conversion, which has been too common. Judgment to come, not the Atonement, is the doctrine preached by the Apostles as the means of conversion; and then, when men " were pricked in their heart," " remission of sins." Even the school in question abstractedly acknowledged the principle, in that their Sermons were wont to consist of two parts; the first, inculcating our lost condition through nature, the second, salvation through the Blood of Christ. Even according to them, the Atonement was not to be preached, until people were supposed to be convinced of their " lost and ruined condition;" which involves the very principle in question.

Any condemnation then of the principle, as " keeping back the blessed doctrine of Atonement"—except when minds are for the time unfit to receive it, when it might harden rather than soften them,—censures not the principle, but one which the author of those Tracts equally condemns. How entirely those Tracts have been misunderstood, has become apparent in reference to one particular Charge, the author having shewn, by aid of parallel columns[a], that all which the Bishop wished him to have said, he had said, and not said, what he wished unsaid. I may use words of his own to myself; " The propositions condemned by the Bishop I not only never expressed or thought of, but disapprove of in the strongest manner as extremely wrong."

Another of these Charges furnishes in a different way a remarkable illustration of the same misunderstanding. The Bishop of Winchester seems to imagine that the principle involves a keeping back of religious truth altogether, not a reverent and holy imparting of it. Hence many of the cases which he quotes from Holy Scripture to disprove the principle, are in fact instances of it; how our Lord *in private* gave a fuller insight into Divine mysteries to those prepared to receive them, as to the eleven after the resurrection, or to the sincere and enquiring Nicode-

[a] A Few Remarks on the Charge of the Lord Bishop of Gloucester and Bristol, on the subject of reserve in communicating religious knowledge as taught in the Tracts for the Times, No. 80 and No. 87, by the writer of those Tracts.

mus; or Himself prepared them before He even declared the truths of nature, as when He "convinced of sin" the woman of Samaria, before He declared to her the spiritual being of God; or how, in public, He veiled the truth before those who were about to "rend" Him, as in that mysterious intimation, " Destroy this temple [b]." It might illustrate these misconceptions further, that the same Bishop supposes[c] the way of teaching recommended in this Tract to be parallel with the dry moral preaching too common in the last century.

In a word, all the Bishops who have blamed these Tracts have blamed but one statement, in a sense not held by the Author, not borne out (one must say) by the tenor of the Tract and of our teaching, and subsequently explained by him[d]. I may say,

[b] "At the first Passover He assumed a right over His Father's House by cleansing the Temple—a declaration [rather, a veiled intimation] of the Divine prerogative of the strongest kind. His discourse with Nicodemus is based upon the doctrine of regeneration—the deepest theological truth. His conversation with the woman of Samaria revealed that ' God is a Spirit'—the most abstract metaphysical truth. We remember how some months before His Crucifixion, He *intimates* the Sacrifice Itself and its object, ' Destroy this temple.' ' The Son of Man must be lifted up.' ' The bread that I give is My Flesh, which I give for the life of the world.' And it was His last care, *immediately before the Ascension*, to enter *with the eleven* into the full explanation of,' &c. Charge of the Bp. of Winchester, p. 31.

[c] Ib. p. 31.

[d] In Tract 87. The Charge of the Bishop of Exeter was delivered before the publication of the second Tract. The Bishop of Gloucester is stated "upon the best authority" to have

without disrespect, that I cannot but regard it as an instance, in which the Bishops have been unconsciously acted upon by current statements and vague accusations, rather than themselves acted on their own dispassionate and mature judgment. Certainly, there is in all a remarkable repetition of the same general statement, " keeping back of the doctrine of the Atonement," and no indication of any acquaintance with the principles of the Tracts themselves.

Yet the treatment of these Tracts which has been thus unhappily countenanced,—being condemned and spoken of lightly, without being considered,—is but one form of that very habit of mind, against which they were directed. The opposition to them originated mostly in the very need of the medicine which it rejected. Had the Tracts been entitled, " On *reverence* in communicating religious knowledge," it would have been a severe condemnation of the error which they now treat more tenderly, but one which could have been less easily eluded. As it is, people have gone off upon a name, and shrunk from the substance. The real aim of those Tracts is to correct irreverence in handling religious truth. And of this there is but too much need. Our age is irreverent; irreverence pervades almost all the discussion of sacred subjects; in speaking and writing alike, people forget of Whom they are

referred only to Tract 80, not being acquainted with Tract 87. (Church Intelligencer, No. 31.)

speaking, Whose words they are using, Whose Mysteries they are handling, about Whose very Nature they are bandying words; they forget themselves and God, and so have been turned against that, which condemned themselves. Profaneness is the very characteristic of the world[e]; but alas! one need not go to the world for absence of reverence; the very handling of the most sacred subjects of human thought in our daily press side by side with the things of this world is irreverent; one cannot read a page of them without being pained by irreverence; one need only think of any one subject, as those which our Church still calls " holy Mysteries,"—what language is used either as to the Romanist doctrine or Catholic truth, when and how, by whom and before whom they are discussed! One can hardly understand how they who hold them to be mysteries can so speak, or they who so speak can retain the sense of their being mysteries. Or to consider again the hard dry way in which the Blessed doctrine of the Atonement has been illustrated or vindicated, until one knows not which was most rationalistic, the defence or (grievous as it is to say) the attack! Or to take lighter cases, how frequent it is, even in the most sacred places, much more in so-called religious meetings, to hear religious truths so spoken of,

[e] There is a fearfully condensed picture (though from the nature of the subject in allusion chiefly) in a thoughtful article in the British Critic, No. 61, p. 237.

that any one must be certain that the speaker is not for the time thinking whereon he is speaking. For myself, when I first learnt the substance of those Tracts, I felt that they conveyed a lesson we all needed, that their teaching, well-weighed, would deepen all our reverence, and teach us, almost all, how much it needed to be deepened. They seemed to come most seasonably also, (one might say, providentially,) at the revival of religious truths, as a warning against bringing them forward, as people are wont, without due reverence to the sacredness of that wherewith they are entrusted, or regard to their own temper of mind, or that of those to whom they declared them. I have since met with many, who entered upon the study of them with minds prejudiced against them by the popular misrepresentations, but I have not met with one, who, (whether he acquiesced or no in all the details,) did not express himself deeply indebted to them. It will not, I trust, seem disrespectful if I express my conviction that our Bishops, had they fully considered *both* these Tracts, would, instead of singling out one topic for condemnation, have recommended their general teaching, as a corrective of so much under which we are now suffering [d].

[d] A valuable analysis of them, and independent testimony to their value, is given by the Rev. H. A. Woodgate, " A Brief Analysis of the Tracts on Reserve in Communicating Religious Knowledge in the Series called Tracts for the Times: with Remarks on the same."

Even as to that Tract, which, perhaps from some few expressions in it, or its original designed indefiniteness on some points, has been most animadverted on, it may be the rather hoped that not the actual interpretation of the Articles in Tract 90, but their supposed tendencies have been censured, since my own vindication of them has, with one exception, escaped censure; and in that one, in addition to the extensive misunderstandings which I have pointed out, language of the Homilies[e] has been censured as much as my own. I must, however, candidly avow my belief, that had there not been a strong, traditional[f] but unauthorized, interpretation in the one direction, which Tract 90 struck at the roots, there would not have been that alarm, which at first certainly prevented an unbiassed view[g]

[e] In that the Homilies speak of " the Sacrament of Matrimony;" the expression has of late been vindicated in the abstract, but not used; the Bishop of Chester condemns it. p. 79.

[f] This Mr. Newman avows it to be his desire to oppose, " I should not be honest if I did not add, that I consider our own Church, on the other hand, to have in it a traditionary system, as well as the Roman, beyond and beside the letter of its formularies, and to be ruled by a spirit far inferior to its own nature. And this traditionary system not only inculcates what I cannot receive, but would exclude any difference of belief from itself. To this exclusive modern system, I desire to oppose myself." Letter to Dr. Jelf, p. 17, 18.

[g] The Bishop of Llandaff, however, kindly observes in reference to this same Tract, " He" [Mr. Newman] " has been, I think, unjustly accused of leaning towards Popery—for his language has been strong and unequivocal in condemning the usurpation,

being taken of it. In one instance, we must gratefully acknowledge, that the Catholic sense of the Articles is explicitly acknowledged, and the judgment only of our Reformers, as being many and revering Catholic Antiquity, is preferred to the judgment of any individual, as to what the Catholic sense is[h]. One general misconception I may yet remove, as though Mr. Newman had set himself systematically to prove that "a person adopting the[i] doctrines of the Council of Trent, with the single exception of the Pope's supremacy, might sincerely and conscientiously sign the Articles of the Church of England." Of this there is no appearance in the Tract itself, nor of any systematic design in it: the allusions to the Council of Trent are incidental only[k], correcting ultra-interpretations of some of its decrees. It may suffice to notice, that as to the most important and difficult

and the corrupt unscriptural tenets of that Church;" on Roman Catholic Errors, p. 87. He points out also that the Tract so far from favouring the *actual* system in the Church of Rome, implies that it is worse than at the Council of Trent. ib.

[h] " Knowing the respect in which our Reformers held Catholic Antiquity, I should believe that they were more likely to have correctly embodied that sense in it [the wording] than I, as an individual, should be, to discover that sense for myself." Bp. of Ripon's Charge, p. 25.

[i] Bp. of Gloucester's Charge, p. 35.

[k] This also is stated by Mr. Newman, " That *while I was writing it* [Tract 90] I was not unwilling to shew that the Decrees of Trent were *but partially*, if at all, committed to *certain* popular errors, I fully grant; but even this I did with reference to others." Postscript to Letter to Dr. Jelf, p. 1.

Decree, that on Transubstantiation, no attempt is made, either to reconcile it with Antiquity or with our Articles. As little ground is there for the conjecture[i], that " the real object of the writer was to prove that the differences in doctrine which separate the Church of England and Rome will upon examination vanish." Any such question the writer has stated[j] to be, in his opinion, unsuited to

[i] " The real object, at which the writer *seems* to be labouring is, &c." ib. p. 36.

[j] " In like manner I have set my face altogether against suggestions which zealous and warm-hearted persons sometimes have made of reviving the project of Archbishop Wake, for considering the differences between ourselves and the foreign Churches with a view to their adjustment. Our business is with ourselves—to make ourselves more holy, more self-denying, more primitive, more worthy our high calling. Let the Church of Rome do the same, and it will come nearer to us, and will cease to be what we one and all mean, when we speak of Rome. To be anxious for a composition of differences, is to begin at the end. Did God visit us with large measures of His grace, and the Roman Catholics also, they would be drawn to us, and would acknowledge our Church as the Catholic Church in this country, and would give up whatever offended and grieved us in their doctrine and worship, and would unite themselves to us. This would be a true union; but political reconciliations are but outward, and hollow, and fallacious. And till they renounce political efforts, and manifest in their public measures the light of holiness and truth, perpetual warfare is our only prospect. It was the prophetic announcement concerning the Elijah of the first Advent, that he should ' turn the hearts of the fathers to the children, and the heart of the children to their fathers.' This is the only change which promises good and is worth an effort." Letter to the Bp. of Oxford, p. 43, 44. " Those who are immediately about me, know that in the interval between the

the present state of the two Communions; both Churches must be other than we are, before the question of union can be healthfully entertained by either.

I have thus, at the risk of wearying your Grace, gone through the main topics of these Charges, in order to shew that even in them it is mostly not our doctrine which is condemned, but, as I said, something which we should equally condemn ourselves; that, when we take more pains to understand one another, unity within our Church is not so hopeless, as amid our distractions it now seems. But although one may see this one's self and so look hopefully onward to a rest for our Church, even if we should have entered first, as we hope, into our own, this will not be the ordinary impression. These Bishops mean to condemn what they think us to be. And what have we to set against all this, why this should not be accounted as the earnest of the voice of those set over us in the Church? While some Bishops, who belong to an opposite school of theology, do condemn what they think is our teaching, others, who were formed in the same general outline of doctrine as ourselves, are thought to condemn us, another condemns us

printing and publication of the Tract, I was engaged in writing some Letters about Romanism in which I spoke of the impossibility of any approach of the English toward the Roman Church, arising out of the present state of the latter, as strongly as I did a year ago, or as I do now in my Letter." Postscript to Letter to Dr. Jelf, p. 1.

in the mass, without apparently knowing any of the details of what we have taught, but thinks that instead of the Church, the Sacraments, repentance, " righteousness, temperance, judgment to come" according unto our works, the whole is a question of the revival of ceremonies, or " the follies of by-gone superstitions[k]," how may not younger or less-disciplined or more ardent minds be well disquieted at the prospect? For ourselves, we had enough in the acquittal, some years past, of our own Bishop. But for the Church at large, what is there to counterbalance all this? Except some kind expressions, some years past, of one Bishop[l], and, in the last year, of another[m], nothing has been said, except what has been lost sight of, as though uttered in extenuation only of censure.

And this is the more aggravated, through the relative position of the two great sections of our Church. Two schemes of doctrine, the Genevan and the Catholic, are, probably for the last time, struggling within our Church; the contest, which has been carried on ever since the Reformation, between the Church and those who parted from her, has now been permitted to be transferred to the Church herself; on the issue hangs the destiny

---

[k] Bp. of Durham, p. 12.

[l] Bishop of Lincoln.

[m] Bp. of Llandaff, on Roman Catholic Errors, p. 87 and note, whose personal kindness the writer especially has gratefully to acknowledge.

of our Church; if human frailty or impatience precipitates not that issue, all will be well, and it will have a peaceful close; yet a decisive issue it must have; the one must in time absorb the other; or, to speak more plainly, the Catholic, as the full truth of God, must, unless it be violently cast out, in time, leaven and absorb into itself whatever is partial and defective; as it has already very extensively. I do not wish to call the attention of your Grace or any other of your Grace's brethren to any defects on the other side. But if every thing is said on the side of supposed excess, nothing of defect; if they are blamed who interpret our Eucharistic Service in its fullest sense by the Liturgies from which it is derived, they are not blamed, who explain away it or our Baptismal Service by the Zuinglian school, or even omit Baptismal prayers, whose plain meaning condemns their system; if they are censured who fill up inadequate statements in our Articles by the teaching of the Church Catholic, they uncensured who pare down the meaning of our Liturgy; they censured who bring up the meaning of our Articles when indefinite to our Liturgy, they uncensured, who bring down the definite meaning of our Liturgy to the lowest interpretation which can be affixed to the Articles; must it not be thought that the sympathies of our Bishops, are with those who are treated thus leniently, against those whom they censure? This has been already felt. In one Diocese, which was becoming more tranquil, and there seemed hopes of a better mutual understanding, thanks were publicly given in one chief place, that the Bishop had from that pulpit denounced our teaching as " another Gospel[n];" in another great city, the people were instructed to look upon the teaching of a portion of the Ministers of their Church, as the teaching of Satan. Would that this were an insulated case!

If this goes on, my Lord, where is it to end? If our own Bishops and others encouraged by them say to us—sore as it is to repeat, they are their own words—" Get thee hence, Satan,"— while those of the Roman Communion pray for us, and invite us, is it not sorely adding to the temptations, I say not of ourselves, but of younger men? The young are guided by their sympathies more than by their convictions; our position is

[n] The Bishop of Gloucester plainly meant to enforce the principle that individual character is no excuse for bringing in error of any kind; " But if an Angel from heaven preach ' any other Gospel than that which we have received' from the Apostles and Evangelists, I trust that he will preach in vain." (p. 38.) He could not have meant what the words would go to, since he had just said; " I am *well* acquainted with some persons, members of my own Diocese, whom report numbers among the supporters of the system which those writers recommend and uphold. And I bear my willing testimony to the *exemplary purity* of their lives, *their doctrine,* and *their opinions.*" p. 37. The Bishop of Calcutta, however, does seem to use those same sad words in their full meaning. p. 43.

altogether an unnatural one; it was never meant, nor did he who first originated the idea of our Tracts, contemplate, that we should stand thus; we never wished to be leaders; he who has been forced into that unenviable eminence loved retirement and obscurity; we wished, as I said, to rouse, at a critical moment, the sense of our Church to the value of a part of her deposit which she was neglecting; our first Tracts were the short abrupt addresses of persons who, when the enemy was upon them, seize the first weapon which comes to hand and discharge it; our more elaborate ones grew under our hands and became such almost without our own will; we formed no system; we did nothing to gather people round ourselves; we besought others (though in vain) to preach in this place on the same doctrines, that those doctrines might not be identified with us; we wished to guide people away from ourselves, and pointed them on, and have been essaying to lead them, to the Ancient Church, in connection with our own; our publications of the Fathers, which had the sanction of your Grace and other your Brethren, had this as its main object, to present the fulness of the Ancient system, in faith and life, apart from modern statements and modern controversies; we forewent much which any of us might have desired to do, in order that the Church might be listened to, not ourselves; in whatever degree we have been made a party, it has been the act of others not our own; we are held together not by party-ties but by our common Faith, and our common object of restoring our Church; we were formed in different ways [n], have retained the character impressed upon each, (which party obliterates,) and, while we hold the same Catholic truths, have, in some cases viewed men and actions differently; we have acted independently, one in this way, the other in that, as to each was given; we have vindicated prominently different portions of the Truth; we have adopted no characteristic practices; have revived nothing in common but the acknowledged practices of our Church; when people are compelled to leave declamation, and name our peculiar tenets, they can find which they can distinguish from those of our chief Divines; we have no title except one given in reproach by our opponents, and which is not unfrequently applied to your Lordships' body as well as to ourselves, whenever your acts bring out the character of the Church more than they approve of, who so designated us. We wish to be merged in our Church, to be nothing but what is of all the highest, Ministers and servants of our

---

[n] I may instance the remarkable history which one, not connected with the Tracts, has given of the way in which his views were lately formed, against his own will; Letter to a Protestant-Catholic, by the Rev. W. Palmer, Fellow of St. Mary Magdalen, where he explains the anathemas which, in the first instance, from an apparent vehemence, gave pain, among others, to myself also.

God in her, " repairers of the breach, restorers of paths to dwell in[o]." But if we are thus singled out from the rest of our Lord's flock, as diseased and tainted sheep, who must be kept separate from the rest, lest we corrupt them; if a mark is thus set upon us and we are disowned, things cannot abide thus. For us, who are elder, it might be easy to retire from the weary strife, if it should be ever necessary, into lay-communion, or seek some other branch of our Church, which would receive us; but for the young, whose feelings are not bound up with their Church by the habits and mercies of many years, and to whom labouring in her service is not become a second nature, an element in our existence, their sympathies will have vent, and, if they find themselves regarded as outcasts from their Church—to a Church they must belong, and they will seek Rome. And yet, my Lord, this would be very miserable; they for whom I speak are not (as I have reason to think has been represented to one of your Lordships) unsubdued wilful young men, who at the first check which they receive from authority, are ready to fly off; it is not they who threaten secession, it is we who venture earnestly to state to your Lordships a secession with which they and we would be alike threatened. Among those, in whose minds serious misgivings have been raised, are not merely what would be

[o] Is. lviii. 12.

ordinarily called, " young men;" there are, one may say, some of the flower of the English Church; persons whose sense of dutifulness binds them to her, who would, to use the language of one of them, " feel it to be of course their duty to abide in her as long as they could." What we fear is not generally a momentary ebullition, but rather lest the thought of seceding from our Church should gradually become familiar to people's minds, and a series of shocks loosen their hold until at last they drop off, almost of themselves, from some cause which in itself seems wholly inadequate, because their grasp had gradually been relaxed before. What we fear is lest a deep despondency about ourselves and our Church come over people's minds, and they abandon her, as thinking her case hopeless; or lest individuals who are removed from the sobering influence of this ancient home of the Church, should become fretted and impatient at these unsympathising condemnations, and the continued harassing of the unseemly strife now carried on under the shelter of your Lordships' names, and losing patience should lose also the guidance vouchsafed to the patient.

What we crave, then, my Lord, is sympathy. While we cannot abandon what we believe to be true, we have ever been ready to acknowledge that prejudice may have been created against the truth by our imperfect modes of stating it. We must sorrowfully feel—there is much shame in making this confession in behalf of others less imperfect than myself, yet all must feel painfully—that had they more of the Blessed Spirit of Truth, their teaching would more approve itself to be truth, since it would appear that it is " not they who speak but the Spirit of their Father which speaketh in" them. In part also a prejudice may have been created against the truths we taught, by our teaching them unsystematically; it has been said of us, that we were ourselves learning while we taught. This which must in some degree be true of all, may have been specially so of some of us; it hardly could be otherwise in recovering any body of doctrines which had been cast into the shade; people are led on step by step, until they in some measure see the whole. Your Grace will excuse my explaining what I mean by reference to myself, of whom one must know most. In writing my Tracts on Holy Baptism,—which I undertook not of my own mind but to rescue a pupil from falling into dissent,—wishing to comment upon all the texts of Holy Scripture relating to it, I was forced upon one, which impresses the character of grievous sin after Baptism. In writing upon it, I kept as much as possible to the language of the Ancient Church, saying little of my own, as fearful to trust myself°. What I wrote, I hope that with

° The same seems to have been the object of a very solemn sermon on the same subject recently published; " Evangelical Repentance" with an Appendix by the Rev. C. Wordsworth, in

deepening years I hold more deeply; and day by day shews me how needful the doctrine is for these times, that without it there can be no thorough restoration of our Church, nor high standard of holiness; but my statement was imperfect, as making no mention of the healing and comforting power of Absolution or the pardoning grace in the Holy Eucharist. I have since endeavoured to remove objections to my statement in my Letter to the Bishop of Oxford, and to supply what was wanting in University and other Sermons; the Tract itself has continued out of print for six years, because I have not had leisure to fill up what was wanting, and would not reprint it in a form in which I felt it to be imperfect. I have not to complain that what I wrote above six years ago still remains matter of animadversion; one is responsible for all one ever did. What I endeavoured to impress was truth, although not exhibited sufficiently in connection with other truth; I have reason even to think that in some cases the very nakedness with which it was first proposed, gave it the more entrance; the sterner voice awakened those, whom softer tones would not have reached: however, it was imperfect; I took advice in what I did; I have since done what I could to prevent a very solemn and Catholic truth, which lies at the

which he considers all the texts, which speak of " repentance," and refers to modern writers also. Its tone makes it one of the cheering signs of these times.

very foundation of repentance in most of us, from being injured by my imperfections; and it is matter of sorrow that some incorrect representation of my original statements, rather than acquaintance with those which I have since put forth, or with my practical teaching, was, in one of the Charges at least, the occasion of the animadversions. Thus, a Catholic truth seems to be objected to, not my imperfections in stating it.

It may naturally seem too much to ask of Bishops, pressed down as they are by their over-weighty Dioceses, to examine what one has spoken of as " nearly [p] one hundred Tracts, which have given occasion for almost an equal number of volumes in reply." But, my Lord, Bishops, in animadverting upon them, are looked upon as passing a sort of judicial sentence; their Charges are not merely pastoral advice to their own Clergy, to avoid such or such a mode of teaching; they are printed and circulated through the whole Church, and are regarded as their solemn opinion on them; they are quoted every where not on the particular points merely on which they touch, but as to the whole body of the teaching of the "Tracts." It is then nothing but simple justice to ask, nothing but what any judge in the passing matters of this world would do, that they should put themselves in possession of the whole subject. It surely is beforehand not improbable that they would find,

[p] Bp. of Durham, p. 15.

that what abstractedly seemed too strongly spoken, or to have a dangerous tendency, is qualified by our other teaching. The " Tracts for the Times" do not claim to be a body of divinity, complete in themselves; they are detached writings on distinct though connected subjects or doctrines, such as " the times" seemed most urgently to require; they do not pretend to exhaust the subjects which they treat on, much less to present them in all their bearings, or (which seems by some in this day to be required) to contain in one the whole body of Divinity, so that whatever is not in any place expressly stated, should therefore be accounted not to be held. Surely, then, within the body of the " Tracts" themselves, not insulated passages of single tracts, but the whole substance must be considered together, by any one who has so solemn an office to perform, as to pronounce what sounds like a judicial sentence. But further, though " the Tracts" were in the first instance mostly anonymous, (the writers, then, as younger men and mostly in no ostensible office in the Church, not wishing to put themselves forward as her advisers,) the chief writers and their other works are now generally known. There is then no ground for judging of them, apart from what the same writers have elsewhere said, and are known to have said. Thus, before these authors are accused of too great tenderness for Romanist errors, it would surely have been well to have examined one thoughtful work, written expressly on the subject of Romanism[o], and certainly one of the ablest vindications of our own position relatively to it. Or, on a specific doctrine—it has been thought that our teaching on sin after Baptism would be " gloomy and cheerless[p]," that it would " tend to rob[q] the Gospel of the Blessed Jesus of much of that assurance of the riches of the goodness and mercy of God in Christ, which is its peculiar message—its glad tidings of great joy—' Come unto Me, all that labour and are heavy laden, and I will give you rest;'" that it would tend to lessen our sense of some sins, because less deadly than others[r]. Now before such condemnation is repeated, it is surely not too much to pray, that Bishops would examine our practical teaching. To speak of writers of the Tracts only, there are now three volumes of Sermons professedly by ourselves, expressly intended to exhibit our teaching practically[s], besides the six volumes printed by Mr. Newman. If our teaching in these is not of the character supposed,— and Mr. Newman has sermons expressly bearing upon the subject,—or again, if the doctrine of the Atonement be not withdrawn from sight, or again,

---

[o] Mr. Newman's Lectures on Romanism and Popular Protestantism.
[p] Bp. of Ripon, p. 20.
[q] Bp. of Exeter, p. 82.
[r] ib. p. 83.
[s] See Preface to Plain Sermons, vol. 1.

since one has written a work on The Passion[t], which I will not trust myself to characterize, but which has already brought a holy peace to aching hearts, and will become one of the standard devotional books of our Church,—it will surely occur to them, at least to set down what they object to, to some imperfection of expression, rather than to unsoundness of doctrine, (which must most forcibly appear in practical teaching;)—perhaps it might lead them to think that the statements had not the meaning which they who censure them, had attached to them.

Another impression might perhaps result from this examination; and our Bishops themselves would be glad to find how small a proportion what they found themselves obliged to object to, bore to the whole mass of teaching. I do not say that these Bishops would acquiesce in, or have considered, all other points of teaching in our Tracts; I only mean, that the points actually animadverted upon—except by those altogether of a distinct school of theology, which itself, until of late years, found little favour in our Church—are both few, and do not touch on any Catholic truth, or any of the essentials of our teaching. They relate mostly to modes of statement, character of language, estimation of another Church, not to the main doctrines themselves. I certainly found with surprise as well as

[t] The Gospel Narrative of our Lord's Passion harmonized, with reflections, by the Rev. Is. Williams.

satisfaction, amid the warnings of these Charges, how little altogether was condemned, and nothing essential; I think that they who are so eager to represent us as condemned, would, if they made the same analysis, think that they had little to boast of. Thus, besides the principle of the exposition of the Articles in Tract 90, the Bishop of Ripon blames my way of speaking of Sin after Baptism (which I have confessed imperfect), Reserve on the doctrine of Atonement, tenderness in speaking of Roman practices, too great strength of language as to tradition. The Bishop of Exeter spoke of the same four points, my own (I must say) compelled statements as to 'Prayers for those departed in the faith and fear of Christ,' which never formed part of our teaching; the sketch of a service in commemoration of Bp. Ken, which certainly was never used by any in common. The Bishop of Gloucester speaks but on Tract 90, on reserve and tradition, although the affliction, in which all must sympathize, may have prevented his acquainting himself with other points as well as our real meaning as to those on which he speaks. Even the Bishop of Winchester, although, estimating us by his school, he must also include the doctrine of Justification, speaks besides only of "reserve," the *mode* of speaking of tradition, language as to the Church of Rome, our own, our Reformers, our formularies, or that he thinks we hold the Sacraments to be " *the only* sources of Divine grace, to the exclusion of any other"—none of these controverting or touching any doctrine we hold—I must add indeed one point, intelligible perhaps on his system, utterly unintelligible to me on the system which he opposes, viz. that our teaching "defaces the brightest glory of the Church, by forgetting the continued presence of her Lord;" whereas in effect the very characteristic of the Catholic system is to bear in mind the Presence of our Lord every where, in the Church, in worship, in Sacraments, in rites, in fast, in festival; it loves the Church, as His body; public worship the rather, because He is then more present; fasts, as fasting with Him; festivals and rites, because they speak of Him; Sacraments, as uniting with Him. It is the contrary naked system which does indeed " deface the glory of the Church," and makes her but an " element of this world," " forgetting the continued Presence of her Lord," in her and with her.

And since this is so, and one may claim without hesitation (though setting up no one as a standard except the Church), that our teaching is more in accordance with the acknowledged Divines of the 17th century,—I would not exclude in this respect even those of the 16th,—than that which opposes it, one may on this ground the rather hope that what is thought defective in us, will not be so spoken against, as to seem to condemn our teaching in its substantial parts. They who brand us with names of heresy have, through unacquaintance doubtless, throughout avoided this question, whether the chief Divines of the 17th century are most with us or with them; of the 16th, they are diligent in pointing out against us the varying and unsatisfactory language on the one Sacrament, but take no heed to the clear and definite language of the same writers on the other; they claim single expressions in the Homilies, the body of Catholic teaching contained therein they neglect. Themselves holding with the Non-Conformists, and having learnt of them rather than of our Liturgy or the writers of our Church, agreeing with the writers neither of the 16th century nor, still less, of the 17th, they would gain a tacit admission for their own system by the condemnation of our's, and, themselves of yesterday in the Church, would condemn us for novel teaching.

And yet, my Lord, whatever our imperfections may be, it will be acknowledged that good service has been done. " Not unto us, O Lord, not unto us, but unto Thy Name be the praise," will be the confession of those who have been the chief agents in this work. They have gladly acknowledged that they sowed the seed on soil which God had prepared, had " made soft with the drops of rain, and blessed the increase of it;" they gladly recognise other men's labours, even when they deem their views imperfect, or in grave points erroneous; but still good service has been done; and since others seem to forget it, and even those who in some degree acknowledge it, seem often not to be aware of any thing beyond matter of outward discipline and order, I may speak of it to your Grace; and that the more, since, as it is already appreciated, I have myself the least portion in it.

A great change then has come over our people; it is recognised on all hands that the Church is stronger; in a great political revolution some years past, her influences seemed to be paralyzed; since that time she has, under circumstances outwardly adverse, been steadily recovering it, and they who oppose her, acknowledged that, at the late crisis, it was her influence which decided it. And in what did that influence exist? Not in canvassing or partizanship, but in the silent power which her increased energy gave her over the minds of men, binding them to her. It were not seemly to speak disparagingly of times gone by; we have too much of them still cleaving to us, and, too probably, faults of our own besides; we had in those days also, men who will ever be remembered with veneration and love; still the tone of doctrine and the standard of life was on the whole low; we dare not blame them; they may have acted up to their standard, better than we to ours; we would rather confess " our sins and the sins of our forefathers," and thank God for having hitherto spared us. " Thy father's dishonour is no glory unto thee[s]." Yet in this spirit it may be confessed, that a

[s] Ecclus. iii. 10,

secular temper came gradually over the Church during the last century, which was but little abated at the earliest part of this, and of which we have too many traces still; in earlier days one never heard of self-denial or any of the harder duties, even when collections were made for objects of charity; " sacrifices" was a name unknown; every thing was on an easy footing[t]; decency and propriety were the standards and substitutes for holiness; daily advancement seemed scarcely contemplated as possible; to live under rule was unthought of; fasting was apparently expiring, and hanging upon the lives of those elder members of families, who yet kept one or two of the most solemn yearly fasts; daily service was being fast given up, even in our towns, for want of worshippers; even in the resorts of those who had leisure, the very service in Lent was often broken in upon, because two or three could not be brought together; in the country Good-Friday itself was in whole districts neglected; Catechizing disused; what discipline we might

[t] " One only Way to life;
 One Faith, delivered once for all;
 One holy Band, endow'd with Heaven's high call;
  One earnest, endless strife;—
 This is the Church th' Eternal fram'd of old.

  Smooth open ways, good store;
  A creed for every clime and age,
 By Mammon's touch new moulded o'er and o'er;
  No cross, no war to wage;—
 This is the Church our earth-dimm'd eyes behold."
   Lyra Apostolica, No. xcviii.

exercise, and training of the young neglected; our people grew wild, and most of what was earnest in the lower ranks fell into dissent. In whole districts, to belong to a new zealous sect was the very badge of spiritual life, to belong to the Church was to be accounted lifeless. Communions were withdrawn from sight, and our "daily bread" offered perhaps twice or thrice in the year; more are thought to have commemorated His Precious Death, in sects who knew of no further blessedness in the Holy Eucharist, than in the Church which taught that thereby "He dwelleth in us and we in Him;" doctrine and practice declined together; the true doctrine was forgotten; the service became cold, and few came; religious fervour seemed to be out of the Church rather than within it; what would now seem almost laxity was then accounted to constitute men "saints;" religion was never spoken of, nor common topics spoken of religiously; our final account seemed to be forgotten among the one sort, in the other, a "judgment according to our works" was denied; measures of duty, teaching, ends, motives, hopes, seemed alike earthly, or, on the other hand, men were called upon to rely upon a Redeemer's Blood, without being taught *how* to "follow the blessed steps of His most holy life;" on one side was a foundation with nothing built thereon, on the other, a lowly building, well perhaps that it was so, since it had no foundation. Even they who professed to be most unworldly, seemed to have their eyes fixed on some mere outward manifestations or haunts of worldliness, to be lopping some " uppermost branches," not laying the axe to the root; expediency was the standard of popular morality; religious education, Church-building and works of charity were at a stand, so that if any one gave on a larger scale, he became a sort of witness against the world; efforts for the conversion of the heathen were carried on more extensively by sects than by the Church; indevotion was shewn by complaints of the length of the service; unspirituality by the continued proposals to alter it. In the state, our empire was our idol; while fifty millions were year by year expended on war, not one five-hundredth could be obtained for one year for a religious purpose; the preferment, as it was called, of the Church was matter of open state-negociation and bribery, so that a Minister of the Crown who disposed of it conscientiously, became, on this ground only, an object of admiration; we were ashamed to own in the presence of our heathen subjects that we were Christians, paid military respect to their idols, and denied our knowledge of our own God; the thought of sending out a Bishop to India produced a panic; he entered it almost as a thief; he who was to bear the banner of the Cross was " obliged to get him by stealth into the city" over which he was to preside, " as people being ashamed steal away when they flee in battle;" at home, a celebrated statesman could venture to make it a ground of objection to a measure, that it would promote " too much religion," and was listened to; our very Clergy seemed often more afraid of " over-much" religion than of over-little; their own claims, when they felt them, they seemed mostly to rest on their education, their birth, their manners, their kindliness, any thing but the Apostolic Commission they bore from God; of their two great sections, the one seemed to maintain the skeleton of a traditional system, holding truth often as a negation of other truth, (as, baptismal regeneration to plead against the necessity of change in life;) the other, despairing that " these dry bones" could " live," betook themselves to a system foreign to our Church, formed themselves in the writings of the Non-conformists, and so were often themselves driven into dissent, finding their teaching akin to it, not to the formularies of the Church. They sympathized more with those without the Church than with those within, and were themselves, as they have sometimes owned, on the very verge of dissent. Of the Sacraments, to use the language of an elder, familiar with this school, " the one was denied, the other regarded as a means of religious excitement." One must even fear that the dislike and disuse of the Athanasian Creed argued a deeper disease than the unwillingness to take up its anathemas, since one heard at the same time of the simplicity of the Christian religion, its reasonableness, in other words, its want of Mystery.

One may recite all this, which is only a specimen of much more that remains untold, though one must recite it with aching heart and shame of face, as they who have been " snatched out of the burning ;" still, since we have been so snatched, it may be recited without fearing that it is the sentence of our condemnation. Even yet it is " the day of small things ;" but since our trust is not in ourselves, but in Him Who hath " given us repentance unto life," we may take courage. Beginnings are being made every where. Nothing is as it should be ; but every thing, we may trust, is set in a course whereby it may hereafter become such. Devotion, charity, self-denial, the three great classes of duties as our Lord enjoins them, are increasing ; our Churches are better attended ; our Communions more frequent, our Communicants increased and more devout ; daily service is creeping even into our villages : whereas the service seemed long, some are now looking back with yearning for the fuller services of the Ancient Church ; the hours, whereby she kept her Lord ever in her eye, are being restored ; the weekly commemoration of His Passion is finding its way among the sons and daughters of even our rich and great ; and, with fasting, simple habits, and more self-denying ways, and charity, are being restored ; Lent and the season of The Passion are more realized; the mysteriousness of our Christian life, as having " by Baptism put on Christ," is more felt; our future account more apprehended and brought to bear upon daily life; the bearing of the Cross more taught, and in some degree practised; repentance and humiliation deepened; obedience and submission more recognised and rendered; designs to God's glory and man's good commenced on a more self-denying scale; the education of the poor and the building of Churches carried on with more individual exertion and sacrifice, even while the efforts and means of Societies are enlarged; nobler plans, like that of some years past for the Metropolitan Churches, the Extension of Education, our Colonial Bishoprics, devised and in part executed, and some of them giving birth to kindred efforts; the privileges bestowed on us in our Church more carried into life[u]; those without, wherever

---

[u] The Bishop of Winchester mentions some of these changes, as a blessing attendant upon the " going forth of the word of God in all its freedom and integrity, building up the individual members of the flock in the principles of our most holy faith, and shielding them with the doctrine and discipline of the Church." Among other points he mentions, " Dissent stayed; the Liturgy more highly appreciated; respect for the ordinances increasingly cultivated; the Sacraments duly estimated; Baptism honoured in the presence of the Church, and the pleading for the mercies of the covenant promised by our Lord Jesus Christ in His Gospel; more frequent biddings to the Holy Communion; fewer refusals; a less chilling negligence, and a return to a better mind on the part of them that are bidden, and an approach

she is planted, in this country, in the United States, and even in Scotland, recognising her more and more as a Church, and coming over to her, not for her respectability in the sight of man, but as the building, the ordinance, the body, of Christ; even foreign Churches, long unknown or estranged from, or even now persecuting us, yet still at least

to something of godly discipline in the Christian family and Christian community; catechetical teaching rendered interesting, and appreciated by parents and children; the rite of confirmation rescued from the disgrace of unmeaning profession or formal ignorance;—the recognition of a purer standard of holiness; of the details of Christian duty; of the obligations of the Divine law; of the doctrine of love to God and man in all its enlarged bearings; a way of holiness opened, of holy worship and of holy conversation." (p. 40, l.) Acknowledging gladly the services of the section of the Church which opposes us, and without, in an unseemly way, contending that these blessings have been ministered by their Author through our hands, one might yet ask who is most likely to have been instrumental in them, they who are reproached for over-valuing Ordinances, the Sacraments, the Church and her discipline, or they who so reproach them? one might ask, in matter of fact, which section of our Church has, on the whole, gone most into the " details of Christian duty" or " the obligations of the Divine law," they who are blamed as " legalists" or they who blame them? by which the services of the Church have been most restored? One might ask in the Bishop's own language, which of the two sections would be likely most to " shield persons with the doctrine and *discipline* of *the Church?*" It is distasteful to say this, but it seems required in justice to our principles not to ourselves, since the Bp. of Durham thinks that all had always been going on well, (Charge, p. 10, 11.) the Bp. of Calcutta that this re-awakening was independent of our principles, (Sermon, p. 61.) both agree that we have been but thwarting it.

beginning to suspect that we are a Church, and to have a respect for us and sympathy with us; and within ourselves, there is, one should trust, on the whole, not self-complacency at our progress, which might mar all, but rather an increasing humiliation; with our renewed life, we seem to have become (as must be, in whatever degree it is a life from God) more conscious of the remaining death, the body of death wherewith we are surrounded; we seem to be looking more longingly back to that high standard, which the Ancient Church had, and to be mourning that we are not like her. Our very distractions are a proof of zeal, though we have not as yet the love, which would enable us to understand each other, and prejudice sometimes seems to deprive us of the very wish to do so, yet it is in many a zeal for God's honour, which will in the end be directed aright, even though for the time it is " ignorantly" opposing the truth, whose features have not been enough disclosed for them to recognise; there is a longing after unity, and prayer for it, to which one must hope it will at length be given.

I said, my Lord, that " we were but one small link in the vast chain of means and effects whereby God is working for His Church what He willeth." I shall not therefore be suspected of claiming for ourselves an undue share in this great work. The change, although more marked of late, was not of yesterday or of the last few years. Spring has not at once followed upon winter; much of the chillness of that past season gradually relaxed. Some of the evils, which I have mentioned as characteristic of it, were lessened long since. The section of the Church, which thinks itself most opposed to us, did much in its day to restore religious earnestness and devotion; much was done in a more tranquil way, by some in your Lordships'[x] station, or by those in our own who handed down to our times the principles now put forward more prominently; we "entered into other men's labours," as others, we trust, will reap where we have sown; during these years also in which we have been employed, we have been all along but working together with others in their different spheres, as writers or Parochial Ministers, holding the same general principles, but formed independently of us, by the Same Lord, Who gave us our work. Still it is acknowledged that many have been stirred up by the writings, which have come forth from this place; the new life which has from Above been infused into our Church, has of late taken a form in accordance with the principles of our Church, as they have been set forth here; persons who as yet stop short of doctrines which in the name of our Church we have taught, still own themselves indebted to us for shewing them the nature of that Church, and teaching

[x] e. g. Bp. Porteus.

them Apostolic order; and since it is said " by their fruits ye shall know them," one may cheerfully appeal to the improved tone in the youth committed to the care of our Mother here, in proof of the value of principles, which have brought forth the fruits of good living, obedience, reverence, devotion.

It is felt by those who do not receive some of our statements of doctrine that we have yet on the whole been working in the line of our Church; let this be acknowledged openly, and we shall not be anxious about the effects of any remarks or censures upon us in detail; we will receive them gratefully; since although founded, we must think, on misapprehension of our teaching, our being misapprehended may teach us humility and caution; they may warn us against deviations, into which if (as we trust) we have not fallen, we may yet guard against more diligently; they may remind us the more that the path of true doctrine also is narrow, so may we seek more lowlily and warily to walk in it. Only, not for our sakes but for the very object which your Lordships have in view, to win those whom you would caution,—may I be permitted to add, that any acknowledgment would seem more gracious and be more effective, if bestowed as thanks for services rendered, rather than as it has mostly been, to take off the edge of some censure?

III. Thus far, my Lord, I have felt myself more at liberty to write fully, because personal explanations are the more allowed, as conveying information which those who make them can alone convey. It may seem, perhaps, less permitted to me, to trouble your Grace upon subjects of the Church which have no immediate relation to ourselves; yet here too, I would wish to be considered as giving your Grace information, as to the effects which a certain course of action might have on a large body of individuals with our Church.

The subject to which I wish to advert is our relation to foreign bodies; and it is right, not to conceal from your Grace that circumstances connected with the plan of sending a Bishop of the English Succession to Jerusalem, have awakened very deep and serious misgivings in the minds of those who can best judge of the state of feeling among us, and, I must add, latterly in my own. Our stability, my Lord, at present seems to depend in great measure, upon our remaining where we are. Many persons, whose minds had become disquieted about our Church, have, even when not set wholly at rest, yet come at least to the result, that unless our Church be committed to any thing wrong, it is their duty to remain within her, and see what God will do for her. They would even think it undutiful to imagine beforehand any case, which would compel them to abandon her, as a child would shrink from contemplating that its parent would commit a sin, which should compel it to leave her roof. I have good hopes, that if no organic change be made in our Church, no authoritative explanation on the wrong side placed upon our Articles, and she be committed to no heresy or fresh schism, though we may have to mourn, as we have mourned, over some sorrowful secessions, yet the main body of our Church will be more stayed within her, as year by year, God's hand more visibly prospers her, and she yields more signs of a living Church. To this end, however, it is of the first importance that men's minds should be at rest; calmness is essential to our seeing the truth, since the Spirit of Truth is the Spirit of peace also, and a disturbed mind cannot reflect Him; but people's minds will not be calm, if things around them seem in a course of change, they know not whither. So long as we simply develope our own Church, and bring out her character more fully, as is the tendency of the Colonial Bishoprics, this is well; it is a sign the more of life. But any step which has a tendency to bring her into relations with foreign un-Catholic bodies, will be unsettling. Any advance to Protestantism will produce a counter-movement towards Romanism.

Your Grace will permit me the rather to explain myself with regard to the new Bishopric at Jerusalem, because I myself at first viewed the plan with interest, having received an erroneous impression with regard to it, and so I may perhaps explain not only the feelings of those who sympathize in it, how far they do sympathize, but what their fears are, who dread it; and this it may be the more desirable for your Grace to know, since it will appear, I imagine, for the most part, that those sympathies and those fears relate to different objects; that the fears have sunk far more deeply and extended more widely than your Grace has been led to imagine; and that others' sympathies are not engaged in that part of the scheme, from which alone any of us fear.

I was then at first led to imagine that there was already a Church of Jewish Converts and of English at Jerusalem, and that the Bishop was to be sent over primarily for their sake. This seemed to me a legitimate object; for since people who spoke different languages, though living together, were allowed by the ancient rule, each to enjoy the blessing of a Bishop, there seemed no reason why Jewish Converts should be obliged to use a ritual in a language they did not understand, or be placed under a Bishop, of another nation and speech; there seemed no reason why the Hebrew Psalms should not be once more sung in a Church at Jerusalem, and those who used the Hebrew ritual, be gathered under a Bishop of their own nation. It was also a thing allowed in early times, that one Bishop should enter into a district nominally in the diocese of another, in order to convert Heathen, whom the other failed to win. Viewed then as a Missionary Bishop, whose office was confined to the Jews, there seemed to me no principle opposed to such an appointment. Again, if Prussians, owing no obedience to the Patriarch of Jerusalem, placed themselves under our Bishop, neither did this (whatever my judgment may have been) seem to me a dangerous measure. I hoped that they would be absorbed into our Church, to which they had united themselves, and gradually imbibe her spirit and be Catholicized. I trusted to the Catholicity of our Church to win those who were brought within the sphere of her influence, the more powerful and the higher principle ever assimilating to itself the weaker and lower. But now that various competent authorities combine to state, that the Congregation at Jerusalem consists of but very few, (more than one traveller has stated its amount at about four,) the case is widely different. The whole is an experiment, and that in so serious a thing as a Christian Church. The mingled Church to be formed under our Bishop, of Lutherans and Jewish converts, has been truly though painfully, designated, " an Experimental Church." And what an experiment! to bring together persons, one knows not whom, sound or unsound, pious or worldly, bound together by no associations, accustomed to no obedience, who on the very Lord's Day have practically but one service[y], and scarcely any through the year besides,

[y] The service in the afternoon is identically the same as the morning, and is attended by different members of the same congregation. Even religious persons, or preachers, where there are

never kneel in the public worship of God, sitting when they sing their hymns, standing when they receive the Holy Eucharist,—under Pastors, *consenting* to receive Episcopal Ordination, but not, as themselves contend, valuing it—if this may even be without profanation,—and make ourselves responsible for them, and exhibit these as specimens of the English Church to the Greek Communion, which has just heard again of us, and is beginning to value us. To think, for the time, only of its effect on the Orthodox Greek communion, (apart from the graver and deeper question of the responsibility we should ourselves incur,) what suspicion must needs be cast upon us, that we thus, in their very presence, sanction bodies whom they have anathematized, not incorporating them into ourselves nor infusing into them our principles, but joined in a sort of outward alliance with them, each pursuing its distinct course, worshipping in its own way, except that their Ministers would receive Episcopal Ordination, and engraft the Thirty-nine Articles on the Confession of Augsburg, without our Catholic Liturgy, whereby to interpret them, and accepting either *in so far as* (quatenus) they individually found them to correspond with *their* views of Holy

more than one in a place, do not think of going to the second service. The writer, many years ago, on attending it, was told by an eminent preacher that it was not meant for him; i. e. the instruction then given was of a simpler sort, for the poor; and there seemed to be no thought that any one could come a second time to Church, but for the instruction.

Scripture. What an outward and unspiritual view of a Church and of Episcopacy would it seem to imply us to hold, who could think that such a juxta-position of discordant elements under the—one cannot say government but the—presidency of our Bishop, could constitute a Church!

It would be making ourselves responsible, in the eyes of Christendom,—not to speak now of the Eye of God,—for bodies different from our own, over whom we should have no influence, of whose faith we have no guarantee, of whose life we have no previous knowledge, except that we know that faith in Germany has been miserably shaken, that the self-discipline which our Church enjoins is there unknown and unthought of.

Again, still to think only of its effects externally to ourselves, we should have no safeguard that the Bishop so sent, or Congregations so formed, shall not proselytize or consent to receive proselytes from the Orthodox Communion. It is not many years, I think, since a report of the Society for the Conversion of the Jews published at the other University spoke of the ill-success in its proposed object, but seemed to think the opportunity of preaching the Gospel to the Greeks no small compensation. The conversion of Jew, Turk, and Orthodox Greek, seemed to them a like object. I know not whether the Church Missionary Society, which your Grace has now sanctioned, have yet withdrawn its Missionaries from the same Church, which it openly acknowledged were opposed by the spiritual authorities, but boasted that they were gladly heard by the people. Similar language has been unhappily and is heard elsewhere. But any attempts at "conversion," or connivance in persons forsaking the orthodox communion wherein they were baptized, besides encouraging sin, must immeasurably delay the prospect of union with that communion. We ourselves know the bitterness of losing our own children, which a rival communion is stealing from us. Are we to think the sorrows of another Mother, when bereaved, less than our own? We should definitely fix our own principles. Our Bishop cannot at once promote union and schism; we cannot at once conciliate the parent, and rob her of her children; be a friend and an enemy. We must either rigidly prescribe to ourselves our own bounds and remain with them, or give up the opening prospect of ultimate union. We cannot treat the Orthodox Greek Church, at once as orthodox and heterodox; orthodox in that we think union justifiable, heterodox, since heresy alone can justify secession. This re-opened intercourse with the East is, as your Grace will feel, a crisis in the history of our Church. It is a wave which may carry us onward, or, if we miss it, it may bruise us sorely and fall on us, instead of landing us on the shore. The union or disunion of the Church for centuries may depend on the wisdom with which this providential opening is employed. If the ways which He makes for us are neglected, we may long essay in vain to attain in our own, what in His would have been easy, since He would "make them plain before our face." In proportion to the greatness of the blessing held out to us, must be our anxiety lest we miss it. It stirs the heart and makes one, like Jacob, almost disbelieve for fear, that such an event as the reunion of our Church with a sound branch of the Church Catholic should be open to us; alas! considering what we actually are, it makes us fear lest it cannot indeed be meant for us, and as though it were not in any temper which we can in this day claim, amid mutual self-complacency, but in weeping and sackcloth and ashes that the breaches of our brotherly union are to be healed. " Joseph made himself known to his brethren and he wept aloud—and he fell upon his brother Benjamin's neck and wept, and Benjamin wept upon his neck. Moreover he kissed all his brethren and wept upon them." But, whether this union may now be hoped, or whether what we witness be but the first pale streaks of such a morning of joy, enough for our eyes to behold, only be the delay not brought about by any errors of our own. Yet in proportion to the value of the gift, may we be sure that Satan will interpose hindrances to our attaining it, that it will be beset with snares.

But this is looking far; and my excuse for

troubling your Grace are our dangers in our own home. Our repose at home, humanly speaking, depends, as I ventured to say, on our remaining as we are. Persons are very sensitive about the character of our Church. They have felt keenly the parallel which Romanists are so fond of making between us and the Donatists. It does not indeed hold, inasmuch as that was a sect which, confined within its petty communion, called itself alone *the* Church, and condemned the Church Universal. We have no Church Universal against us; the Greek Church which has anathematized the Lutherans and Calvinists, has spared us; we have hitherto had the Latin Church against us, although we have not rejected its Communion, but been cast off by it; if we voluntarily add the Eastern, we shall have the whole. Nor must one conceal that there is much of this Donatist temper about individuals, and that the self-satisfied spirit of our people has crept into our Church, and they seem to say to all other Churches, " Stand back, for I am holier than thou." And, amid our intestine divisions, disagreed among ourselves what the doctrines of our Church are, even as to the very Sacrament whereby persons are made members of it, they would make converts to—they know not, at least are not agreed, what! Such proceedings must be very fatal to our humility; they were to that of Rome, when it had far more pretensions than we now have, and had a far more righteous cause, and was the bulwark of the Orthodox Faith. It tended to her fall; and we dare not think that, with our miserable disunion and want of discipline, we may, with her, neglect the Apostolic advice, and " be high-minded" and yet be safe, when she fell. But, immediately, in our own day, any exhibition of ourselves as a proselytizing Church would unsettle many of our own children to a fearful extent. Grasping at the shadow which does not belong to us, we should lose what we already have; we should receive the requital, " as thou hast done, so be it done unto thee," we should receive the reward of the spoiler, and be ourselves spoiled[x].

Another source of danger, strongly felt by persons well acquainted with the East, and whose judgment your Grace would value, is any thought of involving ourselves with Monophysites or any heretical sect. And this is no imaginary danger; if Bishop Heber was deceived, much more might one, who himself was not educated in our Faith, nor trained in our Theology. They are described to us by those who know them, as a subtle people, too well versed in their own unhappy heresy, even as a madman acquires a miserable ingenuity in supporting the one hypothesis upon which his disease turns. The Christian Church has been more than once almost deceived by an ambiguous confession,

---

[x] Is. xxxiii. 1.

and that, when they were exercised by the heresy which was covered by it; how much more readily we, who have been so long spared it! Yet your Grace will readily feel how shocking it would be to be thus brought close within the touch of heresy; you will feel how painfully it would distress men's minds, what a mark it would be against our Church, if she were any way committed to it.

And although one would not confuse the Lutheran body with these heretics, still much danger would result from any step which would tend to identify us with them, or which implied that we adopted their formulæ as our own. I have readily owned that we owe a duty to them; I trust that it is reserved for us, hereafter, safely to supply what is lacking to them, and join them on with ourselves in visible unity with the Church Universal; but to effect this, we must draw them back to ourselves and the Ancient Church, not lean over to them. It has been gladdening to see a partial restoration of Christianity from its prostration at the close of the last, and the beginning of the present century; it has been saddening that it has been but partial; there is more of imperfect life than, fifteen years past, any one would have dared to hope, less of complete soundness. It is probably always so, in Churches and individuals; the scars of our wounds abide, even when we are in a degree restored; some effects of men's sins remain, even after their repentance has long continued. Perfect soundness does not follow quickly upon deep disease. Neologism (as your Grace well knows) had preyed deeply into the very vitals of the German Theology of the last century. A talented writer, who has been one great instrument in its restoration, could say, "If[a] from reading *any* [b] of the more recent periodicals one passes suddenly to those of the beginning of this century, one feels one's self at once in a wholly different atmosphere. *From a battle-field one enters within the still Church-yard.* The sun of 'enlightened times' having once emerged above the horizon, its rays travel in peaceful repose over field and village, and the Theologians[c] had only to survey the bloodless victories. Here and there an old supernaturalist starts up—but the conqueror, in full security, can afford to be generous; old Time with his scythe is ready, as the ally of 'enlightenment,' to lay in the dust the aged orthodox heads of the Church.—Had things remained thus, could Theology have existed on for fifty years, without dying of very weariness[d]?". From this deathsleep, which this

[a] Tholuck, Litterarischer Anzeiger, 1836, No. 15.
[b] i. e. Rationalist or other.
[c] i. e. the then Theologians,—the Rationalists.
[d] Shortly after Gabler is instanced with praise, as an exception to his day, because he was in earnest about something, even in maintaining the truths of natural religion. "The earnestness with which he comes forward [against the Pantheistic Philosophy of Schelling] deserves respect; one sees that he has it really at heart, not to allow 'the principles of

writer describes with such true though indignant irony, Protestant Germany was awakened by another battle-cry, its sufferings in the war of 1813—15. The scourge of Europe brought some humbler and chastened thoughts. Yet even in 1825, a theologian, in recounting the Professors who could any how be considered orthodox,—i. e. those who in any contended for the doctrines of the Gospel or its very truth,—counted, in all Protestant Germany, 17; the miracles of our Lord were still, here and there, explained away by the teachers of youth; some of those in the Old Testament were even ridiculed, both were disbelieved by many who were afterwards to be Preachers. They are denied, to this day, by some of the Professors in Prussia itself. Since that time, the hand of God has indeed been with them; it has been " the Lord's doing, and it is marvellous in our eyes;" but from a state of things when Rationalism ruled with a scarcely-disputed sway, to one in which the full Faith of Nicæa shall be received in its integrity—this were such a mighty change, such fullness of life from such completeness of death, that your Grace may well think it subject of enquiry, not whether the three Creeds still stand in the books of their Confession, but whether they are still confessed from the heart, undisputed and unqualified, as saving truth, in the same sense in which they were and are

natural religion' to be cut away from under him. In this dead time Gabler is altogether a sort of theological character."

in all branches of the Church Catholic. Important as Episcopacy is in the maintenance of what is good, there are, in the present state of the German Protestants, things of far more importance than Episcopacy; Episcopacy might, under God, have saved them from this downfall, but it may not be the first in order, in rearing them up; in order to benefit them at all or not to injure them, it may require a certain character corresponding to it. We have ourselves seen, in the experience of the Scotch Church, how little available the establishment of Episcopacy was, in the absence of certain conditions on the part of those who were to receive it; in its present rise and solid progress, we see its inherent power, amid outward pressure or desertion, where those conditions are found. And yet, to produce this state, it pleased God, as it seemed, almost to undo our work, that He might bring it about in His; He employed what was good in the Scotch Church, as the means of purifying and restoring her; He rent from her all human aid, left her to be trodden under foot of men, to be persecuted by the state, almost forgotten by ourselves; but a silent witness to truths which were fading among us; and now by a century of severe oppression and privation He has moulded our premature work to be the fit instrument of His Providence. Yet Scotland never was what Protestant Germany has been, or is. Unbelief had then never yet organized itself within a body bearing the Name of Christ. God gave us, in this instance, a solemn warning how we imparted His gift. To bestow it at present on the German bodies, may be, indefinitely to retard its healthful or extensive influence. It is not yet longed for. The gift of Episcopacy would be no real gift to them unless they long for it; it is not the piety of one Monarch which can make the people fit to receive it; nor dare we entrust so sacred a deposit to any one; sincerum est nisi vas—; with soundness of faith Episcopacy would be a blessing, without it, it may be a curse; it is perhaps not without some ruling of Providence, that they who once professed their value for Episcopacy, as their faith declined, became indifferent to it, when they might have had it; they may have been withheld from that, which they were not fitted to receive. I myself had reason deeply to value and to love, now many years past, several of those who were employed in the restoration of religion in Prussia; I watched, for some time, with deep interest, though mingled sorrow, the struggles to a better state; every thing of a deeper sort, there as here, tending to restoration,—but there, unhappily, not of a perfect soundness of faith, but of Christianity itself. With much to respect, much to love, there seemed always some flaw. They have but lately recovered Christianity;—rather Christianity and Infidelity in its extremest form of Pantheism, are still struggling for the mastery in the minds of their very teachers,—what they have recovered they have recovered in an imperfect form; in the minds of some of the younger men, (corresponding to what has taken place among ourselves,) a longing for a Church has been awakened; and so we may hope that this comes from the Same Hand; let this be cherished; pray we for its growth; it may be but waiting for some years,— as God is guiding things with His mighty Arm— and we may be fitter to impart, they to receive; we may exhibit more of a model, than, amid our present confusion and disagreement as to the first principles of our Church and our practical contradictions or neglect of them, we now do; they be more in a temper to copy what in us is sound and Catholic, when they see it more fulfilled in life. If, as has been said, " Episcopacy is the principle of stability, maintaining each body in the condition in which it is," the premature gift may be an injury; it may be but a perpetuation of error. There is, at present, even in the sounder part of the Luthero-Calvinist body, not a vestige, among its writers, of the first condition of a sound restoration,—humility; there is rather an arrogant exaltation of their own body, as the Mother of all in the West separate from Rome; an assumed superiority to our Church, not an acknowledgment of their own defects; the few who look for Episcopacy seem to desire it, in order to organize their imperfections, not to correct them; the most religious of their theological organs declare against the Catholic view of it; they distinctly tell us that it is looked upon not as any thing spiritual, but as an outward mechanism; they tell us that the people desire it not; they refute the notion (and with good ground) that any changes recently proposed among themselves are any symptoms of such longing; there has been the wish to extend Presbyterian ordination, where now there is none; no desire of Episcopal[a]. It is for your Grace and your Grace's brethren to consider, how, in such a state of mind, you could, without risk of profanation, entrust a gift of the Holy Ghost, which is undesired, set at nought, repudiated, by those who are to receive it.

But, for ourselves, your Grace will permit me to say, that until—not their mere willingness to receive Episcopacy, but—their soundness is ascertained, it would be very injurious to ourselves, to become the source of a heterodox succession. To become responsible for heterodoxy in others is too much akin to being such ourselves. Our Bishops in the last century required that the Church of the United States should use the Nicene Creed in its devotions, before they would consent to consecrate Bishops for it; this secured, as far as might be, that that Church should believe the Faith which she weekly confessed to Almighty God; mere subscription, as is now spoken of, among those accustomed as the Lutherans have unhappily been,

[a] See Note B at the end.

to express, by subscription, only a partial assent, would not. There is no security that in subscribing the Creeds they would adopt them in the sense of the Church Catholic, not as they were qualified in their own minds. Your Grace will excuse my adding, that any recognition of any Lutheran formula, as that of the Confession of Augsburg, which, while in some points more definite than our own Articles would alone be, still expresses other things unsoundly and implies much more, would have a very distracting effect on the minds of many members of our Church, and indeed is such a measure as one sees not how any portion of our Church, even her highest Order, if they were unhappily agreed, could be justified in taking in the name of the whole Church.

I had ventured to write thus much to your Grace, before the official account of the English Bishopric at Jerusalem was published, and I retain it the rather, as containing a general statement of the views of others and myself, without any reference to the specific statement of your Grace. It is with satisfaction that I find the principles of non-interference with the Orthodox Greek Church are distinctly recognised, all proselytising strictly forbidden[a], the desire of ultimate union expressed,

---

[a] " The Bishop is specially charged not to entrench upon the spiritual rights and liberties of those Churches, but to confine himself to the care of those over whom *they* cannot rightfully claim any jurisdiction." Statement, p. 6. The Church of Rome

" healing of schisms" set forth as an object, a
" longing for a renewal of the ancient affection,"
and this with " ancient and Apostolic Churches"
and consequently not with the heretical bodies.
Your Grace also contemplates the exhibition of
" the spectacle[b] of *a* [one] Church, freed from the
errors [of the heretical bodies] and imperfections
[of ' the ancient Churches of the East'] and holding a pure faith in the unity of the Spirit and in
the bond of peace;" your Grace speaks of subjects
of H. M. The king of Prussia, " joining[c] themselves
to *the* Church so formed at Jerusalem," of " pre-
senting[d] to the observation" of the ancient Churches
of the East " the pattern of *a* Church essentially
scriptural in doctrine, and apostolical in practice."

The object then which your Grace seems to have
at heart is the exhibition of the one English Branch
of the Church Catholic; and to this I conclude that
your Grace hopes that the Prussian congregations
will, if indulged in the use of their own services for
a while, gradually assimilate themselves, and become
one with it. I own I cannot myself be sanguine about
the effects of the exhibition of our English Church,

---

is blamed in the same place for " sowing disorder and dissension
amongst an ill-informed people," which would of course equally
apply to the Missionaries of any Society which should set the
people against its spiritual rulers, much more, seduce it from
them.

[b] Ib. p. 3.
[c] Ib. p. 2.
[d] Ib. p. 6.

until she realizes in practice what your Grace in theory describes and longs that she may be. Amid her notorious neglect of fasting, the infrequency of her Communions, and the neglect of her daily service, I fear she will little impress upon the " ancient Churches of the East" her adherence to the " Apostolic practice," when, in the Holy City, they " held fast to the Apostles' fellowship, and to breaking of bread, and to prayer,—continuing *daily* with one accord in the temple :" I fear, until she become other than for some time she has been, she can be no spectacle of a Church " holding the faith in the unity of the Spirit and in the bond of peace;" at least, although one trusts that there is vivid life, unity and peace seem the last characteristics one should have selected for our Church at home.

Still less, I own, can I see,—even if your Grace were advised, or it were lawful[e], to free the Bishop from those obligations by which he is at present bound,—how the picture of an united Church could be presented by an English and Lutheran congregation, of which the one holds " One Holy Catholic Church, throughout all the world," knit together by its Bishops, as " joints and bands," under its One Head, CHRIST, and joined on by unbroken

---

[e] See the very clear pamphlet, " The Bishopric of the United Church of England and Ireland at Jerusalem considered in a Letter to a Friend," by J. R. Hope, B.C.L. Scholar of Merton, Chancellor of the Diocese of Salisbury.

succession to the Apostles; the other, an indefinite number of Churches [f], hanging together by an agreement [g] in a scheme of doctrine framed by themselves, and modified by the civil power [h]: of which the one holds Confirmation to be the act of the Bishop, the other deems such unnecessary but accepts it for its younger members [i]: the one holds Ordination to be derived from the Apostles; the other, that Presbyters, uncommissioned, may confer it, and that those on whom it has been so conferred, may consecrate the Holy Eucharist: the one recites the Creed of Nicæa, the other has laid it aside [k]: in the one, ancient prayer, the inspired Psalms, and hearing God's Word, are the chief part of their weekly service; in the other, uninspired hymns and preaching, with prayer extempore; the one kneel in prayer, the other not even at the Holy Eucharist: with the one, the Lord's Day is a Holy Day, with the other a holyday: the one receives " the Faith" as

---

[f] Confession of Augsburg, Art. 1. " The Churches among us teach."

[g] " For the true Unity of the Church, it is sufficient to agree as to the doctrine of the Gospel and the administration of the Sacraments." Ib. Art. 7.

[h] As in the union of the Lutheran and Reformed bodies.

[i] " The rite of Confirmation will be administered by the Bishop to the Catechumens of the German Congregations, according to the form used in the English Church." Statement of proceedings, p. 9.

[k] It does not always recite even the Apostles' Creed. See Note B.

" once for all delivered to the saints;" the other, as susceptible of subsequent correction and developement: the one rests her authority and the very titles of her existence on being an Ancient Church, the other boasts itself modern: the one, not founded by man, but descended of that founded on the Day of Pentecost; the other dating itself truly from Luther, and claiming to be the parent of all, not in outward communion with the great Eastern and Western Branches, and so of our own Church by whom it was originally converted: the one recognises[i] and has been recognised[j] by the Ancient Church of the East, the other rejects her and is anathematized by her[k]. Still less is there any hope, that by receiving Ministers ordained by our Bishop, they express any wish to be received into our Church, or become one with her. On the contrary, the divergence must be still greater, since they in whom these discordant elements are found, are each anxious to develope its own peculiar character. Your Grace expresses the hope that this Bishopric " may lead the way to an essential unity of discipline as well as doctrine between our own Church and the less perfectly constituted of the Protestant

---

[i] " Letter commendatory from the most Rev. The Lord Abp. of Canterbury," published in the " Statement of proceedings, &c." p. 17.

[j] See instances in Mr. Palmer on the Church, p. 1. c. 9. sect. 1.

[k] Synod of Bethlehem, A. D. 1672. see at length, Aids to Reflection, &c. by Rev. W. Palmer, Magd. Coll.

Churches of Europe," i.e. that they will be one Church, through the absorption of the Lutherans into our Church, and the reception, on their part, of all those things for lack of which they are at present " imperfect." Their view is wholly different; they look to this same event, only as an aggrandizement of their own body, as " securing to the Evangelical Church of the German nation,"—not as " less perfectly constituted" but—" *as*[1] *the Mother of all Evangelical Confessions*, rights commensurate to its greatness, beside the Latin and Greek Churches;" they look to it as an occasion for developing the German Evangelical Church, according to " *the Confession* "[m], and with *the use of the liturgy*, of that Church;" and not only so, but they look upon the diversities of Christian worship, as immutable, inalienable; such diversities, *among Protestant bodies*, belong to the very principle of unity, and are looked upon as upheld by our Blessed Lord Himself. " The diversities," it is said [n], " of Christian worship, according to tongues and races, and according to the peculiarities and historical developement of each nation—that is to say in the Evangelical Church, are upheld by a higher unity,— the Lord of the Church Himself."

With these respective principles and aims, I see

---

[l] " Prussian State-paper to all the Royal governments," reprinted and translated by Mr. Hope, p. 77.
[m] " Prussian State-paper to all Royal Consistories," ib. p. 76.
[n] Ib. p. 74.

not any hope that the Lutheran emigrants will ever become true members of our Church, or that this outward union of bodies of them under a Bishop of our succession can do other than add one fresh element to our present confusions at home, give another subject of disquiet to those ill at ease, when what we so much need is rest and peace; retard the settlement of those questions among ourselves, on which our mutual misunderstandings are shaking our Church so dangerously; delay indefinitely the very objects we long for,— the conversion of the Jews, and re-union with the Orthodox Church of the East.

A happy pause, I trust, has now been given to our Church; the first step,—which would in itself, I believe (although not without anxieties) command the sympathies of all,—the consecration of a Bishop to represent our ancient British Church in the city of the Holy Sepulchre, has been taken; and although the Church might naturally have looked that so solemn an act should have been done in the name of the whole Church, that if we did send a Bishop to that blessed Place, he might have gone with the longings and prayers of all, not have been sent with the concurrence of five or six of our Bishops only, still, thus far, nothing has been absolutely done, which need in itself cause anxiety. Difficulties seem to have been providentially interposed to arrest things just at this point[n], where they may be done without any compromise of our Church, and safely, if but wisely, executed. We may look with comfort and hope to an act, which again gives us an interest and a portion in the Holy Sepulchre, and unites around it representatives of the three branches of the Church Catholic. For ourselves, (in whom probably there exists a livelier interest in

[n] Mr. Hope's valuable pamphlet shews very solidly, that Bp. Alexander is a Bishop of the United Church of England and Ireland, bound by her Canons, Articles, Rubrics; under canonical obedience to her Metropolitan; that he is prohibited by his oath at Consecration, from ordaining any Clergy except as Clergy of our Church, using her Liturgy, her Catechism, "ministering the doctrine and Sacraments and discipline of Christ as she has received them," receiving those only to the Holy Communion who are "confirmed or ready and desirous to be confirmed." Those, then, admitted into Communion with Bp. Alexander, "must" (to use his words) "come, not as a body, but as individuals; not asserting an independent collective existence, but desiring to be adopted and incorporated into the Church. Their previous baptism he must ascertain to be sufficient; their present doctrines to be, not of this or that form, but in themselves the doctrines of the Church. He must then upon their desire confirm them, as by Canon 60 he is bound to do; and having, by these several acts of the Church wherein he is Bishop, separated and taken them out from their former fellowship, he may admit them to the blessed Eucharist; and in that privilege retain them as long as by doctrines, morals, and liturgical conformity, they remain stedfast in their profession." p. 28, 9. The consecration then of Bp. Alexander is not even a step toward that which the Prussian Government holds out, "a developement" under *our* Bishop, "of the German Evangelical Church, according to *its* confession, and with the use of its Liturgy. It is purely an act for our own Church, and does not in any way connect her with, or commit her to, Lutheranism.

God's ancient people than in any other branch,) there is an immediate office, in gathering them into the One fold, and in ministering to that other people°, who, amid the other manifold workings of His Providence, were directed by Him to call upon us to convert them; and while, as I trust, we obtain a blessing through our labours, we shall be gathered, together with the representatives of the other branches, ready, in His good time,—there, where He was crucified for us,—to sorrow together that we have rent His seamless coat, and pray Him to fulfil His own prayer for us, that we may be one, as He with the Father is One. These, my Lord, are objects, which will win the hearts of our whole Church; in these longings we shall be all one; these will have, we trust, no perils; and the memory of such a beginning, separate from things perilous to our Church, will, when God shall be pleased to ripen it, consecrate in the heart of all, the recollection of your Grace's Episcopate.

IV. To sum up, my Lord; what we long for, not for our own sakes but for that of the Church whom we wish to serve, is, at the least, peace; if it may be, sympathy, and direction. We wish the Church to

---

° The Druzes; originally a branch of the Mohammedans, whose characteristic it is to look forward to the coming of one of the Caliphs whom they believe to have been God Incarnate; a feeling which, when He is "declared to them Whom they ignorantly" look for, might become an earnest longing for Him Who is to come. Their application for some one to teach them the Christian faith, was not to Prussia but to us.

act, not ourselves ; we wish a direction to be given to this mighty movement within our Church, which, swelling as it is, month by month, and day by day, cannot be checked, cannot be overlooked, but may be guided,—not, in the default of others, to be ourselves the persons who are to guide it. We wish to see the Church take it up into itself, not to let it roll on, unrecognised, unguided, and with the risk occasionally of bursting its banks, because pent up too narrowly, and opposed by those who have no office to oppose it, so vehemently. We wish to have the direction of things taken out of our own hands into theirs to whom, in the order of God's Providence, it belongs to direct and guide His Church. Had this been done some years past, much of our present disorders might probably have been avoided; we understand that it is said by some, that the writers of the " Tracts" did good service up to a certain time, but that since they have gone too far. Would we had been recognised then! would that it had been avowed that our teaching was, in its main outlines, the teaching of the Church, so could we never, (as we have against our own will,) been made to have the appearance of a party, or been made to stand out thus prominently from our Church in whose name we taught, or received a sectarian name, in itself a blot upon the Church, in that the name of that writer was given who was led first to vindicate at length the doctrine of our Church and the Creed, then most disputed—Baptismal Regeneration. But they who should have guided, for whatever cause, stood aloof; they looked on, mostly, and let others speak, when they themselves should have been listened to and overruled; they allowed us to be entitled " heretics" for vindicating an article of the Creed, and left it undetermined whether we or they who opposed our teaching, spake the mind of the Church: the Church did not speak, and things, in the chaos of conflicting opinions, rolled onwards; the very conflict required new ground to be taken up; what might have been best reserved, until persons were riper for it, was forced upon us then: it was not the equable advance of the Church, as one mighty army, returning from its captivity under the elements of this world to take possession of its almost forgotten inheritance, it was rather the desultory warfare of individuals, each seizing and maintaining a post, as he saw occasion, inviting who would to follow him, moving some in one direction, some in another, some faster some slower, so that the whole motion, though on the whole with one tendency, and overruled invisibly, we trust, by the One " Captain of the Lord's hosts," has been irregular, disjointed, distracted.

Yet even now, it is not too late, if the same course towards those who have been prominent in this restoration, be not persevered in. My Lord, with respect I may say, it is too late for any mere check. It is not by any warning as to any of our supposed tendencies, or by cautions as to any particular statement, or by silencing any one or more of us, that things can be stayed. When the whole ocean is stirred from its depths, to what end to stay, if we could, a single wave? One, and the chief among us, has, at a critical moment for our Church, been silenced as to that controversy which most endangers it, and in which his writings rendered the most signal service; it was not meant doubtless, but on a sensitive mind it was the natural effect. Have the events of the last ten months given reason to think that we have gained thereby? have things been more as your Lordships wish, because the master-mind was withdrawn? or do the Charges of the last summer seem to have promoted peace? does all which has been going on of late,—in which occasion has been taken of an University Election to vent what was pent up, and strife was but let out, not generated by it,—desecrating and distracting holy seasons and the very Festival of " peace to men of peace" with strife and debate,—does this give hope that we are in the way to cherish mutual love, and gain peace?

This very system, which has now been begun, of procuring lay-addresses from persons who mostly know nothing of the teaching against which they petition, wherein did it originate? The excitement of last spring was gradually subsiding; a great sacrifice had been made to the peace of the Church; he who had originated and they who had cooperated in our " Tracts" had willingly seen them brought to a disgraced close; and we hoped that the Church might accept the offering, and calmly weigh what had been brought forward. Instead of this, the excitement has been ten-fold. The Bishops' Charges have been made the occasion of attacks, too often, alas! from the pulpit, and that in language little fitted for the sanctuary of God, where our Lord is " in the midst" of us. Persons who hate the principles of the Church for their strictness, or for subjecting the individual will, who, with the condemnation of what they hate, mix up ribaldry and profaneness, have still been glad to carry on their unholy warfare under the banner of our Bishops. Those severed from the Church and wishing her destruction, still plead the authority of our Bishops. Thoughtful sermons on sacred things have been noted down and blasphemously commented upon and ridiculed. It is inconceivable what a flood of profaneness has been, in the last few months, poured out upon our unhappy land under the plea of speaking against what such persons have ventured to call "heresy." And all this, through (one must say) blasphemous writing in the worst part of the periodical press, has reached every corner of our land; they who cannot read, hear; they who understand not what they read, still partake of the general agitation; the repose of our once peaceful villages is broken in upon; the most stable part of our population unsettled; the less thoughtful seem to look forwards to some evil which is to come upon them unawares; " we are all," it seems, (to use their own language,) " to become Papists;" and so they are prepared to desert our Church when occasion offers; others are taught to mistrust the Ministers who have been labouring faithfully among them for years: if former negligences are any where repaired, the negligent have the popular cry ready for their plea; the serious and earnest-minded stand aghast, looking in sorrowful perplexity, what all this can mean. Until of late, men of more thoughtful minds were the more stirred to enter into holy Orders, because our gracious Master Himself seemed to be "hiring labourers into His Vineyard," and " giving each his work;" now, some such even shrink back, doubting, and in dismay what our Bishops may do. What wonder, if some are faint-hearted whether our Lord be in the vessel, which is not only so tempest-tost, but whose very shipmen and pilots are so disunited, how or whither to guide her, " neither sun nor stars appearing?"

If this course then avail not, it is time to try some other. I ventured to say, my Lord, that it is too late to try any mere check. It has been a remarkable phænomenon in this crisis of our Church, that the laity, whom checks of this sort would not reach, and for whom they would not be intended, have on the whole embraced these views more uncompromisingly than the Clergy.

One might apply (mostly to the letter) the words of Tertullian[y], "Men cry out that the state is beset, that the Christians are in their fields, in their forts, in their islands. They mourn, as for a loss, that every sex, age, condition, and now even rank, is going over to this"—(so was Christianity itself called)—" sect." Would that, as to too many, his other words did not hold, " And yet they do not by this very means advance their minds to the idea of some good therein hidden: they allow not themselves to conjecture more rightly, they choose not to examine more closely. Here alone is the curiosity of man dull; they love to be ignorant, where others rejoice to know." Yet the very circumstances in the Church which give encouragement, cause anxiety proportionate. From the very first, these views spread with a rapidity which startled us[z]. We then dreaded lest what spread so rapidly should not root deeply. Even at the first, the light seemed to spread like watchfires from mountain-top to top, each who received it conveying it on to another, so that they who struck the first faint spark, knew not how or to whom it was borne onward. The sacred torch passed from hand to hand; their own neither carried nor could withhold it. And now the light has been reflected from hill-top to valley, has pene-

[y] Apol. c. 1.
[z] " There seems to be something judicial in the rapid spread of these opinions." Bp. D. Wilson, Sermon, p. 63.

trated into recesses; abroad, at home, within, without, in palace or cottage; has passed from continent to continent; we see it spread daily, until the whole heaven be kindled; every where opposed, yet finding the more entrance. The indirect influences, as is always the case in all great movements, has been far greater than the direct. It re-appears, here or there, one knows not how. One may say reverently, firmly believing Whose work it is, " It bloweth where It listeth, and thou hearest the sound thereof, but canst not tell whence It cometh, or whither It goeth."

But since this is so, there is the more anxiety as to individual cases, lest persons use wrongly what they have so frequently acquired for themselves without any previous discipline or moral training. We need additional guidance every where, not to risk the withdrawal of any which we have. Our Laity look to be guided by the Clergy, our Clergy by their Bishops, the young by the elder; but if, instead of guidance, our Clergy are but silenced by general admonitions, or warned away from this or that point, or receive but admonitions which sound like condemnation, but which they know not to be founded on any thorough understanding of the views which are condemned, things can but become worse. Our greatest fear is lest, whereas each class might by due method be retained in its own sphere, each being insulated and deprived of its due direction, the whole should become yet more disorganized. There are wants extensively felt which may be satisfied if but ordinances be restored, already provided by the Church, but that unhappily they are fallen into desuetude. There is greater longing for devotion; let our daily prayers, instead of being left to be almost the badge of a section of our Church [z], be countenanced; let the keeping of fasts and festivals, the weekly commemoration of the Passion of our Lord, and the hallowing of Lent, and the cheerful joy of the Pentecostal season, the greater frequency of Communions, the restoration of the Offertory, and its use in the collection of alms for religious ends, be encouraged. There is a greater longing for discipline, for acting under rule, for the comforts of absolution under a burthened conscience; let the "Ministers of God's Word" be encouraged to train themselves to receive those "griefs" when others wish to "open" them, and give them "the benefit of absolution;" and since the godly discipline which our Church yearly laments, cannot yet be restored, at least let it be extended where it can and is desired; let not persons have the temptation (I know such cases) of seeking relief for their consciences in the Roman Communion, because they look for discouragement if they apply to Ministers

---

[z] Persons have been dissuaded from reviving them on this ground. A party-newspaper lately warned against the Wednesday and Friday Service. (Brit. Crit. No. 61, p. 229.) The restoration has even involved severe privation and suffering.

in our own. There are longings for a life more removed from the world and spent in acts of devotion and charity, there is every where much undirected energy which would fain be taught how to do good, but which now wastes itself too often or even does harm, because left to itself; let this be organized;—in a word, let our Church—instead of leaving every one to " do what is right in his own eyes," and herself occupying an easy medium, rather reproving or forbidding those who are too eager than kindling those who are remiss—seek to provide for the manifold wants of her children; be in life what she is in theory and in her Prayer-book; care for lower tempers, yet not neglect the higher; find vents for the various longings which God has infused; guide, not simply repress; train, what, though unformed and undisciplined, is still reality and life; and we shall be a holier, happier, more united Church; less at strife without, because severally more at peace within; less disputatious, because more reverent; understand one another better, because loving more; less suspicious of others, as more suspecting ourselves; less engaged in things which concern us not, because more occupied in what concerns us, our duties, reverence, love, and fear of Almighty God.

Then, my Lord, shall any of us take the station which we had rather have, building up, according to our several offices and talents, our Lord's household, not forced out of our peculiar posts to guide men's minds, because they come to any of us, not finding guidance elsewhere. Let the Catholic teaching of our Church, and her holy practices be put forward, and we shall no longer stand out conspicuous, because we teach or recommend them. Let the unquestionable teaching of our Church, as to her Orders, the Sacraments, the value of good deeds, and Judgment to come according to our works, repentance towards God as well as Faith in our Lord Jesus Christ, fasting, self-discipline, alms, prayer, reverence,—I might say, the contemplation of the Ever-Blessed Trinity, as the End of our life and death, aims, longings, faith, hope, and love,—be inculcated, and a temper of mind will, I trust, be formed, wherein we shall have a holy calm, and may, in peace and godly fear, consider what remains, and, through the Blessed Spirit of peace, understand it and each other.

In the mean time, your Grace will earnestly desire to promote peace. We much need it; while this tumult lasts, people cannot consider any thing calmly; excitement is not the state in which to come to any settled result; these vague suspicions, ready to believe all evil, are no element of that charity which " thinketh none." These idle fears, as if persons, because they recognise what is valuable in another Church, must therefore be ready to abandon that wherein God has placed them, are but so many tares sown by the Enemy to hinder the growth of the good seed. It is but another instance, how people, acting on different principles, must needs at first, (unless they be mutually patient,) misunderstand one another. To those who honour their Church on no other ground than its conformity to their own ideal of excellence, or her superiority to all other branches of the Church, every confession of imperfection would tend to shake their confidence; they understand not the position of those who, feeling that they owe their allegiance to their Church, because she has the Apostolical succession in this land, and God has placed them in her, and in her made them members of His Son, reverence her, as such, and dare not think of forsaking her, so long as they see no proof that she is forsaken of their and her Saviour, " the Saviour of the Body." These may safely take the tone of humility, so that they feel that in confessing the sins of their fathers, they are confessing their own also. A mother is not loved the less, because she has suffered at the hands of strangers[a]. In like way, with regard to

[a] The following thoughtful passage of one of a different school, has been shewn me while writing the above; the writer makes a stronger confession than has perhaps been made lately, yet was not therefore accused of disaffection. "*The Church of England, in its present state, is not fitted for a General Church.* Its secularity must be purged away. We shall hasten that day when Christians shall be of one heart and one mind, if we inculcate the spirit of charity on our respective circles. I have aimed much at this point, and shall push it farther. The rest must be left to Providence. He only can, by unknown means, heal the schisms of the Church, and unite it together as one

our reformation itself. They who can justify their adherence to their Church, only by her inerrancy, and who would be ready to forsake her, if they thought she had done some things amiss, setting up forthwith some sect of their own (as persons continually have done, carrying out their principles[b])—these must needs think any one disaffected to our Church, who admits any blame to have attached to her. Their own affections are not to her, for herself, but as exhibiting their ideal of a Church; if they thought otherwise, they would leave her. And so, supposing others ready to act upon their principles, they cannot understand persons confessing with holy Daniel "for our sins and for the iniquities of our fathers, Jerusalem and Thy people are become a reproach to all that are about us," and yet that they " yearned over her stones and it pitied them to see her in the dust," or with our own Herbert,

> The second Temple could not reach the first;
> And the late Reformation never durst
> Compare with ancient times and purer years,
> But, in the Jews and us, deserveth tears.

and yet live thankfully under it, and in the dim estate of these last times look the more for the Coming of the Lord to His Temple.

external body; and that this will be done, as some think, by persecution, appears highly probable. I see no other means adequate to the end." Cecil's Remains, p. 353.

[b] As, the Plymouth brethren and others recently.

I may say this the rather, my Lord, because, (while every one must acknowledge that there was miserable sin connected with our Reformation,) I myself hope better of the Reformers than some have lately expressed themselves, and readily receive their declaration that they meant to teach what the Church taught, even while they fell into the language of the Zuinglian school[c]. But it is plainly unjust to accuse those who hold otherwise, of disaffection to our Church, since our Church was not the creature of the Reformation, was " not of man nor by man," but is the same city of God, set up for man's salvation, which was originally planted on these shores by Apostles or Apostolic men. Our attachment is to her, not *because of* any changes which she has undergone, though thankful for His Providence and guidance of her, but *amidst* them, as the precious gift of God, the Ark, which however tossed up and down, He has still guided; " a City which hath foundations, whose Builder and Maker" He is; and we are persuaded that, as heretofore, so now, " the rain, and floods, and winds," however permitted to " beat upon" our " house," and even, for the time, to seem to shake it, will but shew the more that her foundations rest upon " the Rock, that is, Christ." Our attachment is to her, such as God by His Providence has formed her or allowed her to become, and to Him we hopefully entrust her and

[c] Especially, Cranmer's Answer to Gardiner.

ourselves in her, not forestalling what He may design with her, nor limiting His wisdom, that she should ever remain as the Reformation left her, nor yet imagining how He may, if so He will, further restore or enlarge her; much less, ourselves seeking in any way to change her outward form; rather praying with good Bp. Andrews that " what is lacking in her may be supplied," and trustful that He Who has guarded her so long, will still keep her from all heresy and schismatic acts, nor allow her confession of the true Faith to be obscured.

If, as we trust, this be granted, there will, I may venture to assure your Lordship, as far as the observation of individuals can extend, be no extensive defection from our Church. It is very remarkable, already, how persons have by conscience or supernatural Providence, been stayed when, humanly speaking, there seemed nothing to withhold them; it is marvellous, in how many ways God has retained persons within our Communion, when they seemed all but lost to her, and has thereby the more shewn that He is present amid what is now going on within her. And, year by year, as the principles of our Church are more restored and acted upon, the life-giving juice will circulate more through this our " choice Vine" and will retain the grapes, which now seem too ready to drop off, or be " plucked[d]" by every

[d] Ps. lxxx.

passer-by; our "broken hedge" will again be restored; our vineyard no more "trodden down" nor "laid waste[e]." It has been the sickly state of our vine, which has parted with its grapes so readily. As holiness is restored, so will the healthy action, which will not cast them off, but ripen them for Him, Who looketh for its fruits. Meanwhile we may have to mourn over the loss of individuals to Romanism, and the more, if unhappily these miserable divisions and hard speeches of one Minister against another be allowed to continue; but let us learn to take them sorrowfully and in patience, as God's chastisements, not in wrath against one another; displeased with ourselves and our actual state and our manifold defects, which bring upon us these tokens of God's displeasure, not wasting ourselves in unchastened disputings, with whom the fault most lies. They are a sore trial to families; they are probably felt most sorely, and most efforts made to prevent them, by those upon whom the unthinking world casts the blame; but it is too probably part of the trial, "the fire and water" through which our afflicted Church is to "pass," before it be "brought out into a wealthy place." Suffering is the very condition of all restoration. The period of restoration, in body or mind or spirit, in individuals or states or Churches, is always the

[e] Is. v.

most critical. The struggle is the sharpest, and the peril and suffering the greatest, when the evil Power is about to yield to the Divine command, and quit the body it has possessed. The evil " spirit cried and rent him sore and came out of him ; and he was as one dead ; insomuch that many said, he is dead. But Jesus took him by the hand, and lifted him up ; and he arose[f]." If we then are sore rent, so that to some it seems as if our Church must be rent asunder, we may be cheered by our very sufferings, and hope the more that Satan " hath" the greater " wrath" with us, " because he knoweth that he hath but a short time ;" we may the more hope that He is about to " take" us " by the hand, lift" us " up, and" we shall "arise." Our Church has been in part un-Catholicized by those who helped in a degree to unsecularize her. As then her former partial restoration was not obtained without the loss of very many of her members and even her Ministers to Dissent, so now it is too likely that some will be lost to Romanism. People can now look back and even calmly contemplate not those losses only, but even Wesleyanism, as an agency permitted by God in the restoration of our Church. And yet it has rent a million of members from our Church in this country ; it is carrying division, wherever the English name is spread, and is degenerating into

---

[f] Mark ix. 26, 27.

developed heresy; even now, though at length giving back very many, it still carries off others, just as, passing from carelessness to more earnest lives, they were in the way to become valuable members of the Church. We can now see that, (amid whatever defects,) religious earnestness has grown, and are thankful for the life vouchsafed to us, though the rent made has been the deepest and sorest since that consequent upon the Reformation. Let those then, who do see that our Church has been, on the whole, gaining, not be disquieted or start back, at these occasional sad losses; rather have we great reason to bless Almighty God, that as yet they have been so few. These mutual suspicions and heart-burnings among ourselves are doing far more harm to our Church, than any losses, however sore. Rather, the losses, which we all feel in common, let us mourn in common before our God; act upon the spirit of the ancient rule, which, before the holy season now approaching, provided for the laying aside all disputes; humble ourselves in common; and these very losses will, by the increase of our humility, turn to our gain: sorely as they wound us, they will be but His health-giving Hand in merciful severity, " purging us, that we may bring forth more fruit."

We need but peace and love, and we shall soon understand each other better than some now think possible; and with renewed union, we should obtain new strength for the mighty purposes, which the good Providence of our God seems to destine for our Church. " Were we at one," it has been felt, " we might do any thing." We do not need fresh limitations of articles, one way or the other; we, whom our common Mother has borne hitherto, may well bear with one another; our Church wants no changes from without; her one need is a holy peace within; mutual toleration, forbearance, " charity," such as she has, at this season, been setting forth to us, " not self-seeking, not easily-provoked, thinking no evil, rejoicing not in iniquity," (as so many now seem,) " but rejoicing in the truth, bearing all things, believing all things, hoping all things, enduring all things." Prayers for unity and peace, with mutual self-restraint and forbearance, will avail more to the healing of our disorders and to the composing of disturbed minds, than any of those measures, which persons, ill-informed as to the truth of things, are now so eager to promote.

Much, very much, depends upon your Lordships. I cannot think that our Church, which has so often been marvellously preserved, will now be abandoned. The Hand of God is so manifestly with her, that I have no misgivings as to the ultimate issue; but though it were too shocking to imagine that her Candlestick should be removed and she cast away, and though her gracious Lord is giving earnests to the contrary, still there may be much present distress and suffering which might be hindered; or we may fall short of the fulness of that blessing which His mercy is holding out to us. The very Presence of that Hand ought to make us the more reverently anxious, how we act in every detail, as it bears more or less upon His work, (since He does allow men to deface and even mar it); we ought to act with the more awe and trembling fear and cautious dread, as being the more vividly in His Presence and " working together with Him." In such spirit would we wish, in patience and mistrust of ourselves, to school ourselves to work; and if (with the respect due to your Grace's brethren as our spiritual Fathers) I may so speak, in proportion to the very greatness of your Office, is the depth of anxiety with which you will doubtless put your hands to a work so holy and of such awful magnitude. The eyes of the whole Church are upon what is going on in ours; East and West are being reunited in sympathy to see what God is doing with us; they who had thought us abandoned to heresy, are beginning to recognise in us the signs of a Church, or have even anticipated that we should become more Catholic than themselves[f]; each day brings its own change with it, leaves some fresh impression, moulds some fresh mind, carries some new convictions, or deepens what was impressed before, brings home somewhere some fresh truth. This late or present storm, so far

[f] This was recently said, (and in a good sense,) in a French sermon.

from uprooting any thing, has but made what it assailed, strike its roots deeper, and shewn thereby the more by Whom that was " planted," which could not be " rooted up." " We live," it has been said, " in years the life of centuries." I said, " we have the eyes of the whole Church upon us ;" we have tokens that we have far more; in the vehemence of the passions roused, the shocking blasphemies with which holy truths are by ungodly men rent and trampled under foot, nay, in our own sad discords and misunderstandings, we may see that there is one " evil eye" upon us for evil; our Church seems to be the very battle-field of evil spirits: in the manifold restorations of our Church, the renewed life infused simultaneously into every branch of her at once, the Catholicity of extent opened for her in all lands, (such as even the Greek Church never had,) contemporaneously with the Catholicity of spirit re-awakened in her; the continued restoration of the children lost in her captivity and widowhood, and (contrary to the acknowledged history of mere sects, which gradually shrink up and decay) her fruitfulness reserved for her age [g]; the increase of her energy and devotedness in proportion to the magnitude of the evils with which in this nation she is surrounded, and with which she has to grapple,—we may see joyfully and thankfully, that there is One compassionate

---

[g] Ps. xcii. 14. " They shall bring forth more fruit in old age."

Eye upon our Church for good. In her, that now seems to have its fulfilment[h], " the waters increased, and bore up the ark, and it was lift up above the earth. And the waters prevailed and were increased greatly upon the earth; and the ark went upon the face of the waters." The swelling of the waters against her seem, we trust, but to raise her the more above the earth and lift her nearer to heaven and her Lord.

At this anxious crisis of our Church, wherein we "are a spectacle to the world and to Angels and to men," have your Lordships been called to your holy station, in the " government of the Church of Christ," where your every word and action is fraught with consequences incalculable; I dare not apprehend that you will not act with the due reverence and caution, when you know how deeply intertwined with the whole frame of our present Church these chords are, upon which you have from time to time touched, and which some, who know not what they are doing, would urge you to pull so vehemently; how many in silence, yet how profoundly, sympathise; how fearfully any mistaken movement might jar through the whole system; what tokens there are that, whoever may have been here or there employed, the whole is the work not of man but of God. I have no fears, but that, as was prayed for you[i], you will " use the authority given to you,

[h] Gen. vii. 17.
[i] Office for the Consecration of Bishops.

not to destruction, but to salvation; not to hurt but to help ; giving, as faithful and wise servants, to the family of God their portion in due season, that you may be at last received into everlasting joy." And for this cause I have ventured thus to speak. On your Lordships, singly in your measure, but much more, were you to act collectively, may depend the well-being of our Church, or the degree of her well-being, during her whole existence.

It is with intense anxiety, in this momentous day, that any one must act who is placed where his actions must have influence; with such anxiety must one watch every act of others, or take each step one's self; with such must I now commit these words, to be heard of men, wishing to weigh all, yet fearful lest with some they leave the impression the very opposite of what I would—how much greater must be your anxiety, on whose high and holy office, in God's Providence, such a weight and load of responsibility now, suddenly, beyond all past times, devolves!

Yet " even hereunto were we called," and " the greater the sufferings, the greater also the consolation." One may look back, with almost faintness of heart, to those more quiet times when the peaceful establishment of the Church in this country, her Cathedrals and Parish Churches, the palaces of her Bishops, the happy homes of her Clergy, to many eyes made her wilderness look like Eden, and her desert like the garden of the

Lord. But those who had their lot in this fair ground and goodly heritage, may well have had misgivings when in the course of the daily services they have read of the labours, the weariness, and painfulness, and daily care of all the Churches, which pressed upon St. Paul; and yet more still when they have dwelt on the account of the Sufferings of which even these are but a faint image, by which the great Shepherd and Bishop of our souls was consecrated to His Everlasting Priesthood. And now that those times are passed away, and it seems likely to be His will that the remainder of our lives should be passed, if not in suffering, yet in manifold and oppressive anxiety, each day bringing its own burden, though with it its own consolation, I trust that "the burden and heat of the day" will be gladlier to us,—if so be we may hope that we are working faithfully in our Lord's Vineyard,—than ever was the freshness and cool of the morning, when we too were yet unworn.

We would not willingly aggravate the heavier portion, which our "fathers in God" will have to bear; nor will they, I trust, (if one may so speak of those "set over us in the Lord,") be surprised at these trials "as though some strange thing had happened to" us, nor think hardly of ourselves as though we had caused them; but rather receive them as a part of that most precious bequest of our Lord to His Church, "the fellowship of His sufferings," and find their consolation, in that their

Office, ever Apostolic in its origin and descent and character and commission, is now again beginning to receive from the Chief Bishop the especial impress of His Cross, the likeness of Apostolic "weariness and painfulness." The solemn words of one of the best and greatest minds[k] our Church has nurtured, and who lived in the beginning of one of her most troubled periods, will, I trust, minister consolation, as well as find an echo, in the hearts of those, who, with your Grace, have been called of God, to "feed the flock of God, which He purchased with His own Blood."

"It seemeth, the Consecration of legal High Priests, so long as they accurately observed the rites and manner prescribed by Moses, did one way or other cost them so dear, that no man which duly weighed the charge laid upon them would be very ambitious of the office. Hence saith our Apostle, 'No man taketh this honour unto himself but he that is called of God as Aaron was[l]:' so likewise Christ took not to Himself this honour to be made an High Priest, but He that said unto Him 'Thou art My Son, this day have I begotten Thee,' put this charge or honour upon Him; against His will questionless, as man, albeit He most obediently submitted Himself to His Father's will, because He had taken the form of a servant upon Him. His Consecration, we may safely avouch, cost Him

[k] Jackson, on the Creed, b. 9. sect. 1, fin.
[l] Heb. v. 4.

dearer than the Consecration of all legal Priests that had been before Him, or of all the Christian Bishops or Prelates which have lived since did or doth them, whether severally or jointly. Never did any man utter those words so truly and sincerely, 'Episcopari nolo,' as He did, or pray so earnestly, that the charge of His Consecration might be mitigated whilst He was in His Agony. But how dear soever His Consecration cost Him, the costs and charges of it, though altogether unknown to us, were recompensed by the purchase which He gained by it: for, as it followeth, 'being thus Consecrated, He became the Author of everlasting salvation to all that obey Him;' and their salvation was and is as pleasant to Him as His sufferings whereby He was Consecrated were for the present distasteful."

May I, however unworthy, be permitted to pray that these things which for the present are distasteful and " grievous," being hallowed by His precious Sufferings, may turn to your endless " profit" and joy.

Your Grace's humble and faithful
servant and son,
E. B. PUSEY.

Christ Church,
Quinquagesima, 1842.

O Lord, who hast taught us that all our doings without charity are nothing worth; send thy Holy

Ghost, and pour into our hearts that most excellent gift of charity, the very bond of peace and of all virtues, without which whosoever liveth is counted dead before Thee: Grant this for Thine only Son Jesus Christ's sake. Amen.[m]

[m] Collect for Quinquagesima Sunday.

NOTES.

Note A, page 58.

Extract from the Bishop of Chester's Charge, attributing the teaching of the "Tracts" to the agency of Satan. (p. 19—22.)

"And here it is impossible not to remark upon the subtle wiles of that Adversary, against whom the Church of Christ is set up, and whose power it is destined to overthrow. His activity is in exact proportion to the activity which is used against him. His vigilance never fails to seize the opportunities which the weakness of man too frequently supplies. No sooner is good seed sown in the field, than tares are found springing up amidst the wheat. Such has been the case throughout the whole history of the Church: and it has been signally and unexpectedly exemplified in the present day, by the favour shewn to notions which might seem inconsistent with the advancement of reason, by the revival of errors, which might have been supposed to be buried for ever."

"To enter upon this subject generally or fully, would be quite incompatible with the limits of a Charge, and to treat it cursorily would not be respectful to my brethren. I shall confine myself to a brief review of two points, in which the interests committed to us are especially concerned."

"The principle by which, in all ages and countries, the power of Satan has been most successfully assailed, and the human heart most strongly actuated, is that of simple reliance on Christ Jesus: simple acceptance of the truth, that He is 'made unto us of God, wisdom, and righteousness, and sanctification, and redemption.' Accordingly, this doctrine, that, lying under God's wrath and condemnation, we are justified by faith in Jesus Christ: this plain and simple truth has uniformly been assailed by every instrument which the enemy could bring to bear against it. From the time when certain men went down from Jerusalem and troubled the Church at Antioch; from the time when Paul had to grieve over the disciples in Galatia, that they were 'removed from the grace of Christ into another gospel, which was not another gospel;' for it was no gospel at all; from the earliest days until now, this has been the point of attack, because on this all depends. We are still experiencing the same and from the same cause."

"Through the merciful providence of God, the true principles of the Gospel were prevailing through the length and breadth of the land, and effects were following which they alone are capable of producing. Meanwhile the enemy is on the watch; knows well where his danger lies; and contrives to cast reproach upon the doctrine which is the hinge of Christian truth and Christian practice; to confound things which ought to be kept distinct; things inherent in man with things extraneous to man; individual duties with vicarious merits; and so to reduce religion to that doubt and uncertainty which never has led, and never will lead, to a consistent course of action."

"It is notorious that this attempt, frequently made, and too often successful, has been renewed in the present day. The Author of our salvation, 'not willing that any should perish, but that all should come to repentance and the knowledge of the truth,' has commanded that the Gospel should be preached to every creature. Those have now risen up who affirm that the doctrine of the Gospel, the propitiation made for sin, is a doctrine too dangerous to be openly disclosed, too mysterious to be generally exhibited; and would thus deprive the sinner at once of his motive to repent, and his comfort in repenting. It has been another part of the same system to involve the article of our justification in obscurity; what has been done for us, and what is to be wrought in us, are confused together; and, practically, man is induced to look to himself, and not to his Redeemer, for acceptance with God."

Yet the Bishop, who could write so painfully, and who, in other passages of his Charge, *seemed* to deny doctrines of our Church and of the Church Catholic, did himself, in the last year, I am informed, deliver an address to those whom he was about to confirm, the whole tone of which was altogether Catholic. It came as a great relief to some of his Clergy, who had been much distressed by his Charge; and furnishes another remarkable instance of what every one conversant with those of an opposite school continually sees—how much of the apparent condemnation of each other arises in misapprehension of what is actually held by either.

Note B, page 127.

Extract from a German Periodical, illustrative of the view taken by the sounder part of the German writers of the introduction of Episcopacy from England.

The following extract is taken from a full article in the "Theologische Studien und Kritiken," a periodical representing the views of a large section of the German theologians, of varying shades of doctrine, (as will appear from the very names of the editors [a],) but, on the whole, those of the middle party of such as are engaged in the work of restoration, with no strong feeling for Lutheranism. The article appeared in October last; it contains no allusion to any domestic plans for the introduction of Episcopacy, but is written with reference to the influence of the opinions now prevailing amongst us, as they bear upon themselves. This object is thus stated by the writer in the opening of the article:

"What is now going on in the English Church is of such sort, as not only to have roused from their repose (so far as they enjoyed it) her own members, and compelled them to decide and take their side for or against, but to claim the attention of those without her, and make them wish thoroughly to understand it. And this is not mere curiosity, as though they who follow those events with eager expectation, were like spectators in a play or a race; in more than one respect, are we concerned ourselves. First, amid whatever manifest differences, there still are not wanting points of contact and analogies between the state of things in both countries. Then also, in England, they have the German-Protestant Church in view, pass judgments upon her, form wishes relatively to us, and would fain point us out our way, and bestow on us what is to promote our well-being. Since then our concerns too are discussed, we may as well assist at the conference."

The writer then explains how the title Anglo-Catholicity designates the movement going on here; and his observations may be serviceable, when people are questioning whether our principles and those of the foreign bodies are the same.

"They wish to claim for the English Church the

---

[a] Drs. Umbreit, Ullman, in union with Drs. Gieseler, Lücke, Nitzsch.

character of Catholicity. The Apostles' Creed contains the article, sanctam Ecclesiam Catholicam; in the Lutheran translation [?] it stands 'a holy Christian Church;' the English translation has kept more faithfully to the original, and in the Common Prayer-book it is, ' the Holy Catholic Church.' This minutia, that this little word 'Catholic' has remained in the Creed, has its weight. Since the Apostles' Creed is recited in each public service in the English Church [b], and repeated by the people after the Minister, not only is the word 'Catholic' retained in a good sense, but there is also maintained a vivid feeling and consciousness of a pervading Unity of this Christian Church, to which they belong. Herewith is an element provided, which, under favourable circumstances, might become a fruitful germ of views, relatively new and amazing, of comprehensive compass, and, in their practical tendency, of no ordinary weight. If, in addition, we take into account, that the English Church, however great store she sets by her quality of a Catholic Church, is yet also essentially a reformed Church, and stands opposed to the Roman-Catholic Church, we come nearer to the specific meaning of Anglo-Catholicity."

The conclusion, above referred to, has immediate reference to a hint in Mr. Biber's "Standard of Catholicity," of the duty incumbent upon these bodies to seek to recover what they had abandoned. However one may lament that the writer considers Episcopacy as something merely outward, yet there is much truth both in what he says of their own condition, and his gentle irony at our insular self-complacency.

" So are our ecclesiastical relations viewed by those of the High Church [the English Church], so are they accounted for; and so do they think that the evil [Rationalism] is to be cured. They hold it the duty and calling of

---

[b] It would seem then, not always in the Lutheran.

their orthodox Church, to undertake the care of the sister branches of the Universal Church, especially when these are in danger of sinking continually deeper in darkness and error. Their notion, in one word, is, that if we would introduce the Episcopal form of Government, and that in such wise, as to have Bishops consecrated by English Bishops, the spiritual authority would be based on its true and safe foundation, and thus would all unbelief and un-Churchism be most effectually suppressed. It is implied, of course, that where now no ordination at all is used, ordination of all Clergy by the Bishops is to be introduced."

" Now then certainly there is an appearance, as though there were not wanting a disposition on our side, to meet half-way the reform-schemes of the High-Church islanders. On the one hand, the institution of Evangelical Bishops does exist in some German states, and, theoretically also, there are some friends of this form of Church-Government, as when Stahl in his recent work on Ecclesiastical Law gives to the Episcopal Government the preference over that by Consistories and Presbyteries. On the other hand, where Ordination is not employed at all, much, on many sides, is said about introducing it."

" But looking more closely, in neither case does the real state of things answer the views and schemes of the High Church. First as to the Episcopate, the Evangelic Bishops in Germany are a creation of the state, by virtue of the principle that the King is Bishop of the Church of his country[b]. The High Church on the contrary, protests formally and solemnly, ' The King can make no Bishop.' The consecration by the Church, and that through the hand of a Bishop who can rightly claim the Apostolic

---

[b] They hold the office also only during pleasure. The king who makes them, can unmake them. " Bishop" among them is a mere title of office.

succession,—this, and this alone, makes a Bishop. The same objection, on the Anglican view, would equally hold good against the theoretical commendation of the Episcopal Government, above spoken of, since all therein maintained was, on grounds of expediency, a relative superiority of the Episcopal over the Presbyterian form of government[c]; whereas, on the Anglican view of Episcopacy as a Divine institution, it is an absolute Essential. Still a step has been made towards an approximation ; and, in the High Church circles, people flatter themselves with the hope that, sooner or later, we shall betake ourselves to the Church of England, and beg of one of the British Successors and Possessors of the Apostolic office, the Church's blessing for German Protestantism; a blessing, which would serve at the same time as the benediction on the spiritual marriage between the English and German Church. In this way a very promising beginning would be made towards raising the English Church into a sort of Rome, a Mother-Church, with the Primacy over Protestant Christendom. Nay, when the Roman Catholic Churches should renounce their errors, and be converted from Romanism to the true and genuine Catholicism, which the English Church, singly and alone, has preserved; when, lastly, the Greek Catholicism of the slavish East, now again renewing its youth, becomes well-disposed to Anglo-Catholicism, then will the whole Christian world be reconciled with the Church of England, and acknowledge her Primacy ; and then, what Irenæus in his time said of Rome, will, in a more excellent, ideal, sense be fulfilled in the English Church. 'Ad hanc Ecclesiam propter potiorem principalitatem necesse est omnem convenire Ecclesiam, hoc est, eos, qui sunt undique fideles,

[c] [Also, as government only, not as a spiritual office, or the channel of spiritual gifts.]

in qua semper ab his, qui sunt undique, conservata est ea, quæ est ab Apostolis, traditio.'"

" The union with the [Roman] Catholic Church is not at present very immediate. The Court has gained the victory; the received opinions in the Catholic world are more Roman than they lately were: and ' an union with Rome, as it is,' say these writers, ' is impossible.' But if we look around us in times past, recollect the Ecclesiastical principles of the Reformation-synods of the 15th century, the Gallican liberties, Justus Febronius and many other maintainers of like views at present, an union of the Catholic Church in this form with the Anglican, does not seem a mere chimera. Did not the Gallican Clergy of the 17th century, stand nearer to an English Bishop than to the Jesuits? witness the thanks of the Gallican Synod of St. Germain's, sent in writing to the English Bishop Bull, for the service which he had rendered the Catholic Church by his defence of the Ante-Nicene fathers against the Jesuit Petavius."

" Until the golden age of the union of our Church with that of England arrives, we remain without Bishops who can claim Apostolical succession; consequently also without real Ordination; for this depends upon a real Episcopacy. In this respect also, the advances on our side are mere appearances. Whoso recommends the introduction of Ordination, where it now exists not, means only to restore a laudable custom, which he expects to work well, not to satisfy an absolute duty, of Divine right. So then we and the Anglo-Catholics are still far enough apart."

" This they may lament. But if they lament for us, I fear they will not have much thanks for it. Who of us could be so minded, as to think that the cure for our religious and Ecclesiastical condition is to be found in the Episcopal Succession and the threefold spiritual consecration? No one of any understanding could look to a remedy, coming in every sense [d] so 'from without,' as a solution of our perplexities. If our theological and philosophical, religious and ecclesiastical, confusions cannot be cured from within, homoiopathically, i. e. by remedies corresponding with the disease, then there is no help for us."

[d] i. e. from a foreign Church and as a thing simply external.

THE END.

BAXTER, PRINTER, OXFORD.